or Ma,

Jessie Spicer Zerner,

our beloved

Angel on Earth

and now

in Heaven.

The Instant Tarot Reader

by Monte Farber & Amy Zerner

A · THOMAS · DUNNE · BOOK

ST. MARTIN'S PRESS
NEW YORK

For information, address St. Martin's Press,
175 Fifth Avenue, New York, NY 10010

Library of Congress Cataloging-in-Publication Data
available on request.

ISBN: 0-312-16681-8

A Thomas Dunne Book

First U.S. Edition published 1997

10 9 8 7 6 5 4

Printed in China by Colorcraft, Ltd.

Authors photographed by Nancy Bundt

Creative consultation / design / production:
APPTEX INTERNATIONAL

CONTENTS

$\mathscr{T}$he cards of the Zerner/Farber Tarot Deck and the details of them that appear in this book are reproductions of seventy-eight mixed media fabric collage tapestries created by Amy Zerner.

The originals are twelve inches wide by twenty-four inches high and incorporate antique and contemporary textiles, laces, trimmings, ribbons and found objects.

3

THE SUIT OF WANDS

MINOR ARCANA

Also known as Fire, Action, Rods, Batons, or Clubs

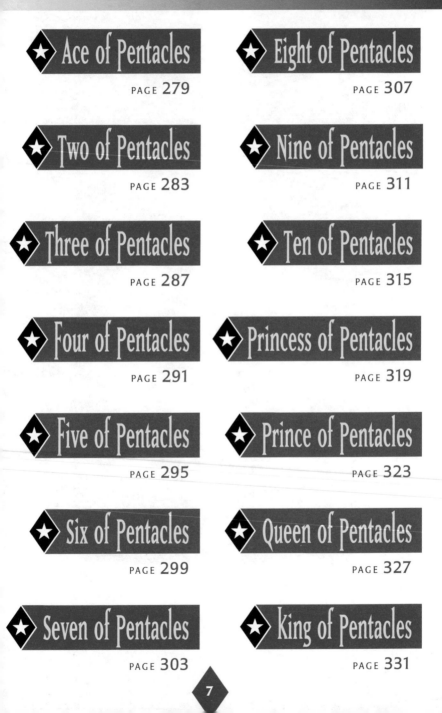
7

$\mathcal{I}$NTRODUCTION

The Instant Tarot Reader

propels the ancient art of the tarot reader into the twenty-first century. As you will soon see, reading tarot cards can be a very powerful, exciting, and enjoyable experience. The gentle, life-affirming guidance contained in the pages of *The Instant Tarot Reader* is as deep and thought-provoking as it is easy and quick to obtain. The included Zerner/Farber deck will always be ready to assist and guide your decisions with its great beauty and timeless wisdom.

When you ask for and receive guidance from the tarot you are performing an ancient ritual—a ritual that is renewed by each new question you bring to it. As you shuffle the cards with your question uppermost in your mind, you become yet another link in an unbroken chain of truth-seekers that stretches far back in time.

For centuries, many European rulers, their courtiers, and their subjects were said to have made regular use of the advice of the great tarot readers of their time. Today, behind the closed doors of board rooms and bedrooms, the rich, the powerful, and the successful still consult the tarot on a regular basis. To paraphrase the late J. P. Morgan's comments about his use of astrology in amassing his vast fortune: "Millionaires don't use tarot cards, billionaires do."

People do not consult the tarot because it is fashionable or because it is an amusing curiosity. They do it because it works for them. It answers their questions and it helps them to make important decisions. Using the power of the tarot gives them a unique advantage over those not bold enough to explore all of their options for gathering and processing information. They consider consulting their tarot cards an integral part of their information "mix." When you use your *Instant Tarot Reader* book and card set, you, too, will be able to instantly enjoy the same advantage hitherto only enjoyed by the rich, the powerful, and the successful. The tarot is not really for the purpose of "fortune telling." However, tarot cards, when interpreted by expert readers like my wife and I, can help you make your fortune.

My name is Monte Farber. My wife, Amy Zerner, and I are the artist and author respectively of *The Enchanted Tarot*, also published by St. Martin's Press in the United States and by various publishers around the world in the English, French, German, Italian, and Portuguese languages. Since 1990, it has introduced hundreds of thousands of people to the fascinating and useful experience of using tarot cards to gain insights into their life and the world around them.

Amy has been my partner since 1974. Together, we have dedicated our lives to using our art to make the timeless truths of ancient systems of knowledge and personal power accessible and useful to everyone here and now in our modern world. We have succeeded in brushing off the "dirt" of centuries of misunderstanding and superstition from the golden treasure contained in all the divinatory arts—especially the tarot. Over time, Amy and I have become the world's foremost designers of personal, interactive divination systems, or, as we like to call them, "spiritual power tools."

Today, there are literally hundreds of tarot decks and many times that number of books claiming to help you to understand the general meanings of the tarot. To really do so, these books require you to spend a great deal of time studying and memorizing the subtle and all-too-often confusing meanings of the seventy-eight cards. Then you must learn the basic meaning of each of the eleven positions of the Celtic Cross layout, the most popular tarot "spread." (The word Celtic is pronounced *Kell-tick*, unless you come from Boston, where they pronounce it *Sell-tick*.)

Incredibly, every single one of these hundreds of other tarot books leaves it up to you to figure out what each of the seventy-eight different cards of the tarot mean in each of the eleven positions of the Celtic Cross spread. Not one of them tells you the exact meaning of each card in every position. No wonder most people who try to learn the tarot give up so quickly!

Only *The Instant Tarot Reader* gives you immediate, easy access to the power of the tarot to guide your life. Only in *The Instant Tarot Reader* will you find the interpretation of each of the seventy-eight cards of the traditional tarot deck in each of the eleven specific positions of the Celtic Cross spread.

Never before in the long history of the tarot has a book like this been available at any price. When you have *The Instant Tarot Reader*, you do not have to spend months or years finding a great teacher and learning how to make practical use of the tarot's ancient truths. When you have *The Instant Tarot Reader*, you have your own personal expert tarot reader on call twenty-four hours a day, seven days a week.

With *The Instant Tarot Reader* book and card set, it is incredibly easy to ask questions and get clear answers to them. You don't have to memorize anything! All you have to do is shuffle the deck and pick the number of tarot cards necessary to ask the type of question you have selected. Then look up your answer in the pages of the main section of this book. Just like an experienced tarot reader, you will form your answer by reading the meaning of each card in each position indicated by the type of reading you have chosen: one-card, three-card, or eleven card Celtic Cross. Every meaning is in the book. It's that simple to become an instant tarot reader.

As all successful people have learned, knowing as much as you can about the conditions that manifest in your life is crucial to making good decisions. As the old saying goes, "Forewarned is forearmed." If things look like they are going to go well for you, then you know to keep doing things the way you have been doing them. If things look like they are not going to go well, then the tarot also can suggest ways to make things go better. As Amy and I always say, poor decision-making is the common denominator of almost all human-caused problems. When you know how to properly read your tarot cards, you can get a whole range of messages designed to give you guidance about future events that may manifest in your life. You will know the correct path to take.

The tarot does not dictate your actions or run your life. Rather than telling you what to do, the cards will put you in touch with how you feel about what is going on in your life and thereby help you to make better decisions. In fact, you can think of *The Instant Tarot Reader* as an executive decision-making tool, a beautiful piece of spiritual exercise equipment, and a unique way for you to improve your decision-making ability.

The Instant Tarot Reader has been designed to enable you to read not only the cards of its included Zerner/Farber deck, but the cards of any of the traditionally structured tarot decks and many of the non-traditional ones as well. Although it has been specially devised to make instant readers out of tarot beginners, even experienced tarot readers can gain new and valuable insights into the tarot by using *The Instant Tarot Reader*.

Each time you do a tarot reading, it is very important that you evaluate what you think and feel about the answer you have gotten. Then make your decisions based on the heightened awareness that the tarot brings to your situation. After a while, you will notice that your intuition and your ability to make decisions, with and without the aid of tarot cards, will improve.

The tarot adds spice to your life, but you cannot live on spice alone. Your free will to make decisions is your "main course." *The Instant Tarot Reader* has been designed to help you to properly access the tarot's ancient truths and put them to use. It is our sincere desire that our creation will help you to better understand your own inner voice and its ability to direct you. We hope you come to know the power that has helped us so that you, too, can make your life all you want it to be. If you approach the tarot with a sense of ceremony, sincerity, and humility, then all may be revealed to you.

$\mathcal{H}$OW TO USE THIS BOOK...

STEP #1:

Select the question which is right for you.

What is on your mind right now? Which question will tell you what you want to know? Look at the list of suggested questions on the following pages and select the one that is closest to the question you want answered.

If you feel like you have too many questions, first ask the one that is the most important. Use the suggested questions to help you simplify and clarify your question.

If you do not have a specific question, just ask the basic question *"Tell me what I need to know for my highest good."* It has been our experience that after someone has seen the tarot cards "lock on" to them and their current situation, they often have many questions.

STEP #2:

Relax. Then repeat your question to yourself as you shuffle your tarot card deck and pick the card(s) needed to answer the type of question you have selected.

Take a deep, luxurious breath and let it out slowly. Now, repeat your question to yourself as you shuffle your deck of tarot cards. If you can, try and visualize your question; see a picture of the situation you are asking about in your mind's eye as you shuffle. Stop shuffling when it feels right to do so. Relax. You are doing fine. If you don't know when to stop shuffling, try shuffling for as long as it takes to ask your question two times.

Next, put the deck down and spread out the cards. Then, one at a time, pick one, three, or eleven cards, according to which section your question falls under. Now lay the cards out face-up following the appropriate card placement diagram.

If your cards come out upside-down, just turn them right side up again. While some readers attach a reversed or weakened meaning to upside-down cards, we do not.

The Instant Tarot Reader

STEP #3:
Look up the meaning of each of the cards you selected in the order that you chose them.

In *The Instant Tarot Reader*, each of the seventy-eight cards of your tarot deck has been interpreted in all eleven positions of the Celtic Cross layout. We also use several of those interpretations to answer the one-card and three-card readings.

To interpret a one-card reading, use the *Index to the Individual Meanings of the Tarot Cards* (starting on page 2) to look up the page where all eleven meanings of the card you have chosen are listed. Then, read the Answer whose number corresponds to the Answer for the type of question you asked as shown in the *Suggested Questions* on the next pages.

To interpret a three-card reading, use the *Index* to look up the meanings of the first card you picked. Then read the meaning which corresponds to the first Answer number listed below the type of question you asked. Then find the correct meanings for the second and third card you picked, as indicated.

To interpret the Celtic Cross reading, turn to the page where the meanings of the first card you picked are listed. Then read Answer number 1 for that card. Then turn to the page where the meanings of the second card you picked are listed and read Answer number 2 for that card. Do the same thing for the remaining nine cards of your reading, making sure that the Answer number you are reading for each card continues to be the same as the position number of the card in your Celtic Cross reading.

It is wise to put a time frame on most tarot readings, but it is crucial to put a time frame on your Celtic Cross reading. When you do a Celtic Cross reading, you will pick a card that describes conditions you can expect to encounter in the near future and another to describe conditions you can expect to encounter in the more distant future. If the next three to six weeks is your time frame, then the last card of your Celtic Cross reading, Position 11, THE OUTCOME, represents conditions you can expect to encounter in three to six weeks and the card in Position 7, WHAT IS BEFORE YOU, will represent conditions you can expect to encounter in three to six days. If the time frame of your Celtic Cross question is three to six months, then Position 11, THE OUTCOME, represents conditions you can expect in three to six months and Position 7, WHAT IS BEFORE YOU, represents conditions you can expect in three to six weeks.

$\mathcal{S}$UGGESTED QUESTIONS TO ASK

IF YOUR QUESTIONS IS:	YOUR ANSWER IS:
Tell me what I need to know about… *(today's events, my partner, my child, my relative, my meeting, my date, my class, my test, etc.)* **for my highest good.**	**1 YOU** FOR THE CARD YOU HAVE CHOSEN
Give me a message about *(my finances, my friend, my family member, my partner, etc.).*	**2 WHAT SURROUNDS YOU** FOR THE CARD YOU HAVE CHOSEN
What is blocking me from attaining my goal?	**3 WHAT BLOCKS YOU** FOR THE CARD YOU HAVE CHOSEN
What should I keep in mind as I try to *(find true love, get a more satisfying job, make more money, deal with rejection, find more free time, etc.).*	**4 YOUR FOUNDATION** FOR THE CARD YOU HAVE CHOSEN

IF YOUR QUESTIONS IS:

What aspect of life shall I meditate on today?

YOUR ANSWER IS:

6 WHAT CROWNS YOU

FOR THE CARD YOU HAVE CHOSEN

IF YOUR QUESTIONS IS:

How am I perceived by the other person(s) involved in my situation?

YOUR ANSWER IS:

9 HOW OTHERS SEE YOU

FOR THE CARD YOU HAVE CHOSEN

IF YOUR QUESTIONS IS:

What will be the outcome of

(my actions, this meeting, an event, etc.)?

YOUR ANSWER IS:

11 THE OUTCOME

FOR THE CARD YOU HAVE CHOSEN

EXAMPLE

QUESTION:

Give me a message about my finances.

READ ANSWER:

2 WHAT SURROUNDS YOU

FOR THE CARD YOU HAVE CHOSEN—Nine of Pentacles

(see page 311)

Nine of Pentacles

IF YOUR QUESTIONS IS:

READ ANSWER:

What are the past, present, and future conditions of

*(my relationship with...,
my situation regarding..., etc.)?*

PAST   PRESENT   FUTURE

THE FIRST CARD YOU HAVE CHOSEN

| 5 | **WHAT IS BEHIND YOU** |

REPRESENTS YOUR PAST.

THE SECOND CARD YOU HAVE CHOSEN

| 2 | **WHAT SURROUNDS YOU** |

REPRESENTS YOUR PRESENT.

THE THIRD CARD YOU HAVE CHOSEN

| 7 | **WHAT IS BEFORE YOU** |

REPRESENTS YOUR FUTURE.

IF YOUR QUESTIONS IS:

READ ANSWER:

What will be the effect of

(this person, place, situation, etc.)

on my mind, body, and spirit?

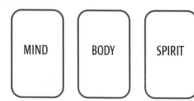

MIND   BODY   SPIRIT

THE FIRST CARD YOU HAVE CHOSEN

| 4 | **YOUR FOUNDATION** |

REPRESENTS YOUR MIND.

THE SECOND CARD YOU HAVE CHOSEN

| 7 | **WHAT IS BEFORE YOU** |

REPRESENTS YOUR BODY.

THE THIRD CARD YOU HAVE CHOSEN

| 6 | **WHAT CROWNS YOU** |

REPRESENTS YOUR SPIRIT.

IF YOUR QUESTIONS IS:

READ ANSWER:

What
(attitude, belief, life lesson, etc.)

do I need to work on mentally, physically, and spiritually?

| MENTAL | PHYSICAL | SPIRITUAL |

THE FIRST CARD YOU HAVE CHOSEN

10 YOUR HOPES AND FEARS

REPRESENTS YOUR MENTAL LESSON.

THE SECOND CARD YOU HAVE CHOSEN

8 HOW TO PRESENT YOURSELF

REPRESENTS YOUR PHYSICAL LESSON.

THE THIRD CARD YOU HAVE CHOSEN

6 WHAT CROWNS YOU

REPRESENTS YOUR SPIRITUAL LESSON.

EXAMPLE

QUESTION:

PAST

PRESENT

FUTURE

What are the past, present, and future conditions of my relationship with my mother?

Eight of Pentacles

Six of Wands

Three of Hearts

READ ANSWERS:

5 WHAT IS BEHIND YOU

FOR THE CARD YOU HAVE CHOSEN—

Eight of Pentacles
(see page 307)

2 WHAT SURROUNDS YOU

FOR THE CARD YOU HAVE CHOSEN—

Six of Wands
(see page 131)

7 WHAT IS BEFORE YOU

FOR THE CARD YOU HAVE CHOSEN—

Three of Hearts
(see page 231)

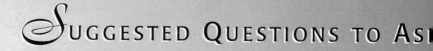

In the Celtic Cross 11-card reading, the numbers represent the position in the card layout and the sequence in which you select the cards for your reading.

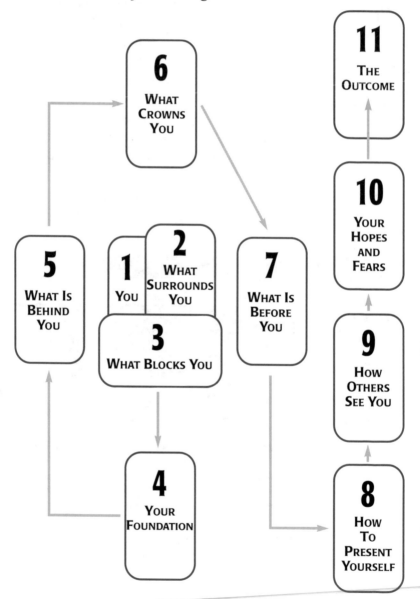

6 What Crowns You

11 The Outcome

5 What Is Behind You

1 You

2 What Surrounds You

3 What Blocks You

7 What Is Before You

10 Your Hopes and Fears

9 How Others See You

4 Your Foundation

8 How To Present Yourself

IF YOUR QUESTION IS:

Give me guidance about

(my life path, my partner, my children, my love life, my work, my financial situation, my living conditions, achieving my goal, etc.)

and how condition will progress over the next three to six

(hours, days, weeks, or months).

YOUR 11 CARD ANSWER IS:

FOR POSITION #1—THE FIRST CARD YOU'VE CHOSEN—READ

1 You

THIS POSITION REPRESENTS **YOUR PLACE IN YOUR SITUATION AND WHAT YOU NEED TO REALIZE YOUR INNERMOST DESIRES** REGARDING THE QUESTION YOU HAVE ASKED.

FOR POSITION #2—THE SECOND CARD YOU'VE CHOSEN—READ

2 WHAT SURROUNDS YOU

THIS POSITION REPRESENTS **THE CONDITIONS SURROUNDING YOU REGARDING THE QUESTION YOU HAVE ASKED**. IF THE ANSWER YOU HAVE RECEIVED IS HARMONIOUS, THEN YOU ARE IN A SUPPORTIVE ATMOSPHERE.

FOR POSITION #3—THE THIRD CARD YOU'VE CHOSEN—READ

3 WHAT BLOCKS YOU

THIS POSITION REPRESENTS **AN IMBALANCE THAT MAY PREVENT YOU FROM ACHIEVING THE OUTCOMES INDICATED IN POSITIONS #7 AND #11 OF YOUR READING**. IT CAN ALSO REPRESENT WHAT IS CONFUSING TO YOU.

continued on next page

FOR POSITION #4—THE FOURTH CARD YOU'VE CHOSEN—READ

4 YOUR FOUNDATION

THIS POSITION REPRESENTS **A FUNDAMENTAL ISSUE WHICH CAN GIVE YOU THE STRENGTH AND SECURITY NECESSARY** TO ACCOMPLISH YOUR GOAL.

FOR POSITION #5—THE FIFTH CARD YOU'VE CHOSEN—READ

5 WHAT IS BEHIND YOU

THIS POSITION REPRESENTS **PAST ACTIONS AND INFLUENCES WHICH HAVE BROUGHT THINGS TO BE THE WAY THEY ARE NOW**. IT CAN ALSO REPRESENT **PEOPLE, IDEAS, AND CONDITIONS** THAT ARE PASSING OUT OF YOUR LIFE.

FOR POSITION #6—THE SIXTH CARD YOU'VE CHOSEN—READ

6 WHAT CROWNS YOU

THIS POSITION REPRESENTS **THE SPIRITUAL GOAL YOU MUST WORK TOWARD** IN ORDER TO ATTAIN WHAT YOU DESIRE. IT CONTAINS A VISUALIZATION EXERCISE TO HELP YOU DO SO.

FOR POSITION #7—THE SEVENTH CARD YOU'VE CHOSEN—READ

7 WHAT IS BEFORE YOU

THIS POSITION REPRESENTS **THE CONDITIONS YOU CAN EXPECT TO ENCOUNTER IN THE NEAR-TERM FUTURE**, IN EITHER THREE TO SIX HOURS, DAYS, OR WEEKS DEPENDING ON THE TIME FRAME YOU HAVE CHOSEN.

continued on next page

FOR POSITION #8—THE EIGHTH CARD YOU'VE CHOSEN—READ

8 HOW TO PRESENT YOURSELF

THIS POSITION REPRESENTS **HOW YOU SHOULD CONDUCT YOURSELF IN ORDER TO BEST ACHIEVE YOUR GOAL**. DO SO KNOWING FULL WELL THERE IS A RISK THAT OTHERS MAY MISINTERPRET YOUR ACTIONS.

FOR POSITION #9—THE NINTH CARD YOU'VE CHOSEN—READ

9 HOW OTHERS SEE YOU

THIS POSITION REPRESENTS **HOW PEOPLE IMPORTANT TO YOUR SITUATION SEE YOU IN RELATION TO THE QUESTION YOU ARE ASKING**. IT MAY BE VERY DIFFERENT FROM POSITION #8.

FOR POSITION #10—THE TENTH CARD YOU'VE CHOSEN—READ

10 YOUR HOPES AND FEARS

THIS POSITION REPRESENTS **A DEEP-SEATED FEAR YOU HAVE THAT YOU MAY NOT BE AWARE OF**. IT MAY ALSO REPRESENT **THE HOPES AND FEARS YOU HAVE ABOUT THE WAY YOUR LIFE MAY CHANGE** IF YOU ATTAIN YOUR GOAL.

FOR POSITION #11—THE ELEVENTH CARD YOU'VE CHOSEN—READ

11 THE OUTCOME

THIS POSITION REPRESENTS **THE CONDITIONS YOU CAN EXPECT TO ENCOUNTER IN THE LONG-TERM FUTURE**, IN EITHER THREE TO SIX DAYS, WEEKS, OR MONTHS, DEPENDING ON THE TIME FRAME YOU HAVE CHOSEN.

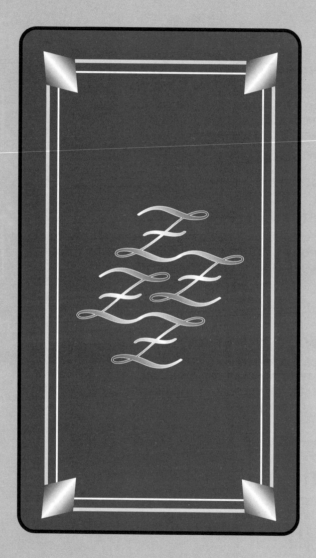

0 The Fool

Trust

◆ The Fool:

Trust

① You

You need to trust that you are a spirit born into flesh to enjoy life and grow in experience. Take a chance and see what happens. Be as open as a child. Risk seeming a bit foolish, naive or optimistic. A sense of humor is vital.

② What Surrounds You

You are surrounded by forces that require and support trust, innocence, and adventure. Focus on the present moment with child-like wonder. Decide what spirituality means. A foolish person may help or need help.

③ What Blocks You

Trust, or a lack of it, blocks progress. Too much, or put in the wrong places, insures disaster. Lack of faith robs potential allies of support and your spirit of determination. Acting foolish, naive or reckless wastes time.

YOUR FOUNDATION

4

Crucial to this situation is trusting that innocence, faith and truth will triumph. A sense of humor is crucial, too. Do not over-analyze or search for hidden meanings. Balance the innocence of youth with the wisdom of years.

WHAT IS BEHIND YOU

5

The time for innocence, foolishness or naivete is past, but it has brought things to where they are now. You know too much now to act dumb or ignore the reality of the situation. Trust must be earned. Do not look back.

WHAT CROWNS YOU

6

It would be good to trust and go on a merry adventure, letting go of all worries. Visualize yourself as a spiritual being, a child descended from worldly and divine forces that guide and protect you from harm.

WHAT IS BEFORE YOU

7

You will soon encounter or have to act as a person who knows how to trust and inspire trust. A major new cycle or adventure will begin. Look at each event as if for the first time. Enjoy and learn from going with the flow.

YOUR PERSONA

8

Present yourself as being as trusting and innocent as a new-born child. Have no fear. Look at the situation as if for the first time. Display your sense of humor and insist that others not take themselves too seriously.

How Others See You

Others see you as a trusting, playful, innocent person who seems unconcerned about the consequences of your actions. You go with the flow. To some you appear fearless. To others you seem unsophisticated or foolishly naive.

Your Hopes and Fears

You hope to be free from the mundane responsibilities, worries and cares of daily living, but fear that you may do something foolish and ruin everything that has come before. You may fear, or fear for, a foolish person.

The Outcome

You will encounter or have to act as a person who knows how to trust and inspire trust. A major new cycle or adventure will begin. Look at each event as if for the first time. Enjoy and learn from it. Go with the flow.

Energy

1 ◆ The Magician:

Energy

1

YOU

You need to personally manipulate things to turn your desires into your reality. Tap the infinite energy of the universe with visualization. Inventory your resources. Use them to manifest the creative control you seek.

2

WHAT SURROUNDS YOU

You are surrounded by a highly charged atmosphere controlled by forces greater than yourself. Their considerable energies can help you if you acknowledge their power. There is magic in the air.

3

WHAT BLOCKS YOU

Willfulness, refusing needed help, or the inability to use your power to make things happen the way you want them to blocks progress. Depending on magic when logic and hard work is needed wastes time. Refusing to see the magic in life is equally counter-productive.

Your Foundation

Crucial to this situation is your ability to identify and use all resources at your disposal to make things happen your way. Tap the infinite energy of the universe with visualization. Acknowledge the source of your power and gifts.

What is Behind You

A time of great accomplishment is passing. Energy and talent have been demonstrated and "magic" has been made. The lessons of this time can be used and built upon to speed progress. A powerful person's influence is waning.

What Crowns You

It would be good to focus available energies to accomplish your goals. Visualize seven energy centers running from the base of your spine to the top of your head. See and feel them pulling in infinite energy from the universe.

What is Before You

You will soon encounter or have to act as a person who knows how to exert creative control to make things happen your way. You may discover energy and resources that help you resolve your situation favorably.

Your Persona

Present yourself as though you know how to use your energy and resources to make things go your way, as if by magic. If you cannot act as the leader, you would do better to act alone. Use the power of visualization.

How Others See You

Others appreciate your energy, intelligence, skill and ability to produce results, as if by magic. Those who want things to stay as they are and maintain exclusive control may resist your efforts to do things your way.

Your Hopes and Fears

You hope you are clever and skillful enough to transform your situation into the way you want it to be, but fear you may not be able to. You may fear your power or have forgotten you are a co-creator of the universe. You may fear the seemingly magical aspects of life.

The Outcome

You will soon encounter or have to act as a person who knows how to exert creative control to make things happen your way. You may discover energy and resources that help you resolve your situation favorably. You may learn the power of visualization to help you manifest your dreams.

2 The High Priestess

Intuition

◆ 2 The High Priestess:

Intuition

YOU

You need to become more aware, receptive, intuitive and even psychic. To do so, know you must get your ego out of the way and let forces of a higher power work through you. Learn to let chaos work for you.

WHAT SURROUNDS YOU

You are surrounded by mystery. Powerful forces show you what is happening beneath the surface. Secrets are revealed. Let intuition reveal meanings behind words and deeds. Learn how chaos can benefit you.

WHAT BLOCKS YOU

Mysterious forces block progress. You may be too passive or relying on intuition and prayer when more logic and hard work are needed. Or you may be denying that intuition is as important as the mind. A quiet person may be the problem.

YOUR FOUNDATION

Crucial to this situation is your willingness to trust intuition and the other unseen forces that affect your life. Great power is gained by listening to others and to your inner voice. An intuitive or psychic person can be a great help.

WHAT IS BEHIND YOU

Spirituality and the knowledge of unseen forces that affect you—or the lack of it—has caused things to be as they are. The time of chaos or passive acceptance of fate is over. An intuitive person's influence may be waning.

WHAT CROWNS YOU

It would be good to accomplish your goal through the power of your intuition. Visualize your situation resolving itself effortlessly, as though guided by benevolent, unseen forces. Know that these forces are real.

WHAT IS BEFORE YOU

You will soon reach a new level of spiritual awareness. You may realize your intuition's power. You may see things are as they should be for your highest good and greatest joy. An intuitive or psychic person may be important.

YOUR PERSONA

Present yourself as someone who is considerate of others' feelings and is respectful of intuitive information and the chaos theory. Be quiet and receptive. Show that sometimes intuition must take precedence over logic.

How Others See You

Others see you as intuitive and deeply spiritual. Some think you are mysterious and powerful because you seem connected to forces much more powerful than your own. Chaos does not seem to affect you like other people.

Your Hopes and Fears

You hope you can follow your intuition, but fear you cannot. Unless you test its ability to direct your life, you cannot hope to become more intuitive and spiritual. You may fear chaos will overwhelm you.

The Outcome

You will reach a new level of spiritual awareness. You may realize your intuition's power. You may see things are as they should be for your highest good and greatest joy. An intuitive or psychic person may be important.

$\diamond$ 3 $\diamond$ The Empress

Creativity

3 ◆ The Empress:

Creativity

YOU

1

You need to give birth to something that has never been. To do so, tap your creative potential. Be as gentle to yourself and your new creation as you would be to an infant. Enjoy the riches of nature and the natural world.

WHAT SURROUNDS YOU

2

Surrounding you is the potential to enjoy the abundance, beauty and joy of the material world. Creativity is priceless now. Something new is being born. This is a fertile time. A creative person can be of great help to you.

WHAT BLOCKS YOU

3

Sensuality, or a lack of it, blocks progress. There must be a balanced focus on the beauty and pleasures of the material world. Your creativity must find adequate expression. Idealizing or denigrating motherhood or the ways of nature may be a problem.

YOUR FOUNDATION

4

Crucial to this situation is your ability to create something that has never been before. Allow nature's bounteous beauty to inspire and show you how to make all dreams real. A nurturing, creative person may be important.

WHAT IS BEHIND YOU

5

Your ability to respond creatively to life's challenges in the past has brought you to where you are now. Your situation is of your own creation. A maternal or creative person's influence on you may be weakening.

WHAT CROWNS YOU

6

It would be good to have the blessings of a nurturing, unconditionally loving maternal figure. Visualize her giving you a life of love, peace, security, beauty and creativity. Allow yourself to feel it envelope you.

WHAT IS BEFORE YOU

7

You will soon experience a period of great creativity or productivity that will help you make a dream come true. Help is close at hand, possibly in the form of a nurturing, creative and talented person. You may become one.

YOUR PERSONA

8

Present yourself as a creative person. Show you want to give life to something that has never been. Demonstrate the ability to solve problems while keeping the interests of all in mind. Be nurturing, caring and loving.

How Others See You

9

Others see you as a creative person. You seem nurturing, caring and ready to give birth to an important new concept. Your love of nature is such that natural forces seem to support your efforts. Many think you are an artist.

Your Hopes and Fears

10

You may long to nurture or be nurtured but fear it will not work out for you. Problems with your mother may be the reason. You may fear the birth of a new project. You may fear, or fear for, a creative person or a maternal figure.

The Outcome

11

Your creative efforts will be recognized and bear fruit. You may know and enjoy many of the ways that heaven exists on earth. Help is close at hand, possibly in the form of a nurturing, creative and talented person. You, yourself, may become one.

4 ◇ The Emperor

Achievement

◆ 4 The Emperor:

Achievement

1

YOU

You need to be recognized as a strong, imposing figure of unquestioned achievement and authority. Focus your attention completely on your goal. You must not reveal your real plans, feelings or weaknesses. Status is vital.

2

WHAT SURROUNDS YOU

You are surrounded by ambitious plans and the potential to gain power over others. You are closely connected with an authority figure, for good or ill. Logic wins out over emotion. Status and achievement are vital now.

3

WHAT BLOCKS YOU

Achievement, or a lack of it, blocks progress. You may not have the proper credentials or respect. Or you are relying on logic, leverage or power when humility would serve you best. An authority figure may be the problem.

YOUR FOUNDATION

Crucial to your situation is your attitude toward power, authority, ambition and self-esteem. The issue of proper credentials and outward signs of achievement will come into play. An authority figure may be important.

WHAT IS BEHIND YOU

A past encounter with the duties and responsibilities of a person of power and authority have brought things to where they now stand. Let past successes empower you now. An authority figure's power is waning.

WHAT CROWNS YOU

It would be good to achieve the status of an authority figure. Visualize someone you respect greatly helping you increase your power and status and helping you reach your goal. Adapt their methods to your situation.

WHAT IS BEFORE YOU

Your power or status will soon improve significantly, possibly with the help of an established authority figure. You may put together the resources to accomplish great things. You may become recognized as an authority.

YOUR PERSONA

Present yourself as a leader of leaders. Assert yourself and take charge. Be calm and reasonable to gain the trust of all concerned. Show what you know, not how you feel. Make sure past achievements are recognized.

How Others See You

Those who value achievement see you as a charismatic leader, a pioneer whose innovation and dedication has produced something of great value. Others see you as cold and willing to do anything to gain power and status.

Your Hopes and Fears

You hope to be a respected authority figure, but fear to take charge and accept the responsibilities that come with the job. Problems with your father may be the reason. You may fear, or fear for, an authority figure.

The Outcome

Your power or status will improve significantly, possibly with the help of an established authority figure. You may put together the resources to accomplish great things. You may become recognized as an authority.

5 ⟩ The Hierophant

Tradition

5 ◆ The Heirophant:

Tradition

1

YOU

You need to be a teacher who passes on the wisdom of the past. To do so, act sure, serene and merciful as you learn and teach proven techniques and traditions. A spiritual practice requires study.

2

WHAT SURROUNDS YOU

The energies around you are supportive, but to make the best of them you must show the value of established procedures, rules and traditions, and try to work within the system. Cultural or religious models are important.

3

WHAT BLOCKS YOU

Tradition, or a lack of it, blocks progress. Tradition, ritual and ceremony can be used, but should not be abused. Lack of tradition leads to moral decay. A cultural or religious model may be difficult to emulate or may cause other problems.

4 YOUR FOUNDATION

Crucial to this situation is your attitude toward established rules, teachings and techniques. A solid grounding in moral principles can get you through turbulent times. A religious or cultural model may be important.

5 WHAT IS BEHIND YOU

Past educational experience, cultural and religious teachings and stereotypes, or the repression of individual expression has brought things to where they are now. Its influence must be recognized and dealt with.

6 WHAT CROWNS YOU

It would be good to receive the blessings and approval of your family and the established social order. Visualize them all approving and supporting your efforts as they realize the ways your actions fit with cultural mores.

7 WHAT IS BEFORE YOU

You will soon offer or be offered advice, comfort or support from a source wise beyond years. You may reunite with some person or thing whose value you knew after its loss. You may know the power of a religious or cultural model or become one in some way.

8 YOUR PERSONA

Present yourself as a dedicated and disciplined practitioner of proven techniques and a defender of traditional teachings. Go by the book. Do not be afraid to lay down the law. Be a model of cultural and religious mores.

How Others See You

Those who value stability, tradition and morality see you as someone who is wise beyond your years—steady, serene and merciful. Others may see you as overly dogmatic and a representative of outmoded ways of being.

Your Hopes and Fears

You hope to join forces with and gain the resources and approval of the establishment, but fear receiving it may interfere with your originality and individual spirit. You may fear, or fear for, a cultural stereotype or fear becoming one yourself.

The Outcome

You will offer or be offered advice, comfort or support from a source wise beyond years. You may reunite with some person or thing whose value you knew after its loss. You may know the power of a religious or cultural model or become one in some way.

Attraction

6 The Lovers

◆ 6 ◆ The Lovers:

Attraction

1

YOU

You need to choose wisely between two or more equally attractive allurements. Know that only if you feel satisfied with who and what you are right now will you choose wisely. Get in touch with what is truly attractive to you.

2

WHAT SURROUNDS YOU

Energies around you require a choice be made between the status quo and the new. There may be a new romance or some other attraction in the air. If you feel satisfied with who and what you are, you will choose wisely.

3

WHAT BLOCKS YOU

The inability to choose wisely blocks progress. Do not be too picky or indiscriminate in your choices of what is attractive. Affections may be misplaced. Good decision making can and must be developed.

YOUR FOUNDATION

Crucial to this situation is your ability to decide between what you have and what you think you want. Dissatisfaction with what you have may reflect dissatisfaction with who you think you are. Outer attractions reflect inner needs.

WHAT IS BEHIND YOU

The time for making a very important decision may be passing. Make your choice soon or a decision may be imposed upon you. The effects of a love affair, attraction or other desire from the past may be waning.

WHAT CROWNS YOU

It would be good to be attracted to the correct decisions in this matter. Visualize yourself as satisfied with who and what you are right now. When you feel confident, make your choice and abide by the decision.

WHAT IS BEFORE YOU

You will soon be faced with a major decision. It may involve a love affair or other attraction. It may be a choice between what you have and what you think you want. If you are satisfied within yourself, you will choose wisely.

YOUR PERSONA

Present yourself as desirous of doing what is best for your greatest good. Affirm your right to control your destiny. Let others know you are considering all your options. Show others what you find attractive.

How Others See You

Others see you as infatuated with someone or something. Most see you as otherwise dissatisfied and tempted by the promise of the new. Some see you as a romantic looking to find truth and beauty through things outside yourself.

Your Hopes and Fears

You think you are dissatisfied with the way things are and hope you will make the right decisions to change it, but you fear losing the good parts of what you now have. You may fear the anguish of a love affair.

The Outcome

You will soon be faced with a major decision. It may involve a love affair or other attraction. It may be a choice between what you have and what you think you want. If you are satisfied within yourself, you will choose wisely.

Determination

7 The Chariot

7 The Chariot:

Determination

1 YOU

You need to focus completely, seize the time, get in the race and win it. Cultivate the ability to withstand the rigors of what is required. Striving towards your goal can be as satisfying as attaining it. You need to be strong.

2 WHAT SURROUNDS YOU

A great event tries to draw you into its excitement. The path to victory is near. There are many resources around you and available for use. You have an air of self-confidence. Make a determined drive toward victory.

3 WHAT BLOCKS YOU

Lack of self-confidence and ambition, or focusing too much on the race blocks progress. An attitude about competition must change. You may have transportation problems. A determination may go against you.

Your Foundation

Crucial to this situation is the strength of your determination, self-confidence and organizational ability. Examine your attitude toward the competitive side of life. Transportation should be functional and available.

What is Behind You

The influence of a contest is waning. Win, lose or draw, it was an important test of your determination, self-confidence and organizational ability. If you learned from it, you won. Complete control is no longer vital.

What Crowns You

It would be good to be able to avoid being distracted and win the goal you know you are capable of attaining. Visualize yourself as a champion whose determination is unwavering. Feel the thrill of the race to sweet victory.

What is Before You

You will soon focus single-mindedly on attaining an important goal. Harness your will-power, self-control and self-confidence, and you will win. Determination will make itself known. Transportation will be important.

Your Persona

Present yourself as a determined, brave, self-confident, take-charge kind of person who will focus single-mindedly on the goal at hand until victory is won. Show you love the drive toward your goal as much as the win.

How Others See You

9

Others see you as determined and a winner, brave and self-confident. Those uncomfortable with drive and ambition may see you as unemotional, aggressive, controlling and fixated on winning at all costs.

Your Hopes and Fears

10

You hope that striving to attain your goal will result in the attaining of it, but fear the demands success will require of you. You may fear that victory is fleeting and the race goes on. You may fear losing control of yourself or others.

The Outcome

11

You will soon focus single-mindedly on attaining an important goal. By harnessing your will-power, self-control and self-confidence, you will win. Determination will make itself known. Transportation will be important.

8 ◆ Strength

Brave Heart

◆ ⁸ The Strength:

Brave Heart

1

YOU

You need to develop true strength. To do so, balance the aspects of you that are human, animal and divine. It may seem impossible, but love, kindness and a brave heart can bring them into balance.

2

WHAT SURROUNDS YOU

You are in a supportive and harmonious atmosphere. There is great spiritual, mental and physical strength around you that you can use if you would only have faith it is in you, too. A brave heart goes on despite fear.

3

WHAT BLOCKS YOU

An imbalance between your carnal desires and your spiritual knowledge blocks progress. Do not deny that your inner dialogue has great influence over your outer reality. A brave heart goes on despite fear.

Your Foundation

Crucial to this situation is your ability to maintain a balance between carnal desires and what is best for the good of all. A hero/ine is as afraid as a coward but a brave heart goes on despite fear.

What is Behind You

In the past you demonstrated the ability to be strong. Your calm, balanced approach—a mixture of love and the resolve to do what is right—should be remembered and used now. A brave heart goes on despite fear.

What Crowns You

It would be good to balance the conflict between spirituality and carnal desires. Visualize them on two pans of a scale being brought into balance through love and perseverance. A brave heart goes on despite fear.

What is Before You

You will soon accomplish with love what force cannot. You will calm fears with courage and perseverance. You may encounter, or become an example of, true strength and bravery. A brave heart goes on despite fear.

Your Persona

Present yourself as one who knows the difference between kindness and weakness. Demonstrate that you know how to persevere and exert control with a loving hand. A brave heart goes on despite fear.

How Others See You

Others see you as strong, courageous and kind. You seem to have conquered your fears and weaknesses and attained the most valuable of strengths: a brave heart.

Your Hopes and Fears

You hope you are strong enough to overcome your fears and weaknesses but fear you are not. You may fear you can never be spiritual as long as you have carnal desires. You can. A brave heart goes on despite fear.

The Outcome

The power of love will triumph over force, coercion and extremism. Faith may be strengthened and the desired outcome may be obtained. You may know what heroism is. You may encounter, or become an example of, true strength and bravery.

9 The Hermit

Introspection

◆ 9 The Hermit:

Introspection

YOU

You need to develop the true power of a master. To do so, be content to be alone or with only those on your level. Do not waste time and energy on those not ready or not worthy. Introspection is required for self-mastery.

WHAT SURROUNDS YOU

You are surrounded by sources of good advice but you must seek them out—they may not come to you. Get out of your routine and use introspection for self-mastery. An older or eccentric person may help or need help.

WHAT BLOCKS YOU

Introspection, or a lack of it, blocks progress. You may be too distant from others or think relationships are not for you. Or you need isolation from the violence or craziness of daily life. An older or eccentric person may be the problem.

4 YOUR FOUNDATION

Crucial to this situation is your ability to avoid snares and distractions of all kinds. Though others may not understand, you must walk your own path. Dealing with the introspection and mastery of the aged is vital.

5 WHAT IS BEHIND YOU

In the past, you withdrew your energies and devoted them to your own interests and pursuits. Introspection and the quest for self-mastery has readied you for this time. The influence of an older person may be waning.

6 WHAT CROWNS YOU

It would be good to withdraw your energies for awhile to devote yourself to finding peace inside yourself and not in the outer world. Visualize yourself in a protective hermit's cave. Feel your introspection produce self-mastery.

7 WHAT IS BEFORE YOU

Energy may soon be withdrawn from the situation or a new path revealed. To follow it requires total attention and dedication. Interest in external events may wane. An eccentric or older person may become important.

8 YOUR PERSONA

Present yourself as an introspective, experienced teacher who keeps secrets because real wisdom is not for every ear. Show you do not need anything from anyone. Do not fear to act eccentric or "too old."

How Others See You

Others see you as introspective. To most you seem mature, experienced, deliberate and someone who does not suffer fools gladly. Some may dismiss you as eccentric, too old or one who avoids all involvement.

Your Hopes and Fears

You hope introspection will help you attain wisdom and mastery but fear what silent introspection would reveal. You may fear being considered eccentric or too old. You may fear aging or fear for the aged.

The Outcome

Introspection will lead to maturity and self-reliance. Mastery may be attained. You may want to follow a leader or path that requires total concentration. An eccentric or older person may become important.

Cycles

The Wheel of Fortune

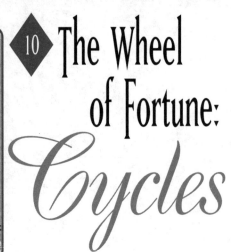

10 ◆ The Wheel of Fortune: *Cycles*

YOU

1

You need to be as lucky as you are skilled, maybe even more so in this instance. Luck comes most often when opportunity, preparation and skill meet. Study the various arts and sciences devoted to cycles and timing.

WHAT SURROUNDS YOU

2

You are in the right time and place to accomplish great things. What seems like "luck" may be good karma returning. Troubles may be bad karma being worked off. You are reaping what you have shown.

WHAT BLOCKS YOU

3

Changing cycles block progress. Your problems may appear to be bad luck but are the result of misunderstood or negative past actions coming back to haunt you. Life, like luck, has cycles. You may be too free-wheeling or trying to tempt fate.

4 YOUR FOUNDATION

Crucial to this situation is how you understand the cycles of your life. Your present situation is the karmic payback of seeds you have sown. Accept responsibility for where you are.

5 WHAT IS BEHIND YOU

The time of danger and opportunities born of karmic payback is over. You are entering a new cycle cleansed of the influence of past actions. It is time to make your own luck Your free-wheeling days may be over.

6 WHAT CROWNS YOU

It would be good to balance past karma that is adversely affecting your present situation. Visualize yourself sincerely apologizing to those you have wronged and them accepting it. You must forgive yourself, too.

7 WHAT IS BEFORE YOU

You will soon be required to take a chance. It may seem to depend on luck or fate but is the result of past karma you have sown coming back as part of a natural cycle. Luck is the meeting of opportunity, preparation and skill.

8 YOUR PERSONA

Present yourself as one lucky enough to be aware of and planning for life's cycles. Show you take responsibility for your life's progress. Display a willingness to take a chance. Do not fear to appear too free-wheeling.

How Others See You

Some see you as getting the reward you richly deserve. Others see you as unpredictable, but basically a lucky and optimistic risk-taker willing to bet your life on getting to the top. A few may think you are a "loose cannon."

Your Hopes and Fears

You hope the Wheel of Fortune will turn in your favor but fear it will not. You may fear the regularity of cycles or taking a chance. You may fear the consequences of past actions or you may fear you do not deserve luck. You may fear, or fear for, a free-wheeling person.

The Outcome

You will reap what you have sown. If you have prepared well and behaved honorably, this is a time of success. Knowledge of cycles increases your responsibilities. Luck is the meeting of opportunity, preparation and skill.

11 ⟩ Justice

Truth

11 Justice: *Truth*

 1

YOU

You need to know and speak the truth and perceive it in the words and deeds of others. Be fair and just with all and you will soon be able to detect dishonesty in yourself and others. Learn the rules that govern what you are involved with.

 2

WHAT SURROUNDS YOU

You are in a place where reason and balance can make it possible for all to cope with each other's viewpoints. The desire to see justice done can enable truth to prevail over fear. Laws and lawyers may be important now.

 3

WHAT BLOCKS YOU

Truth, or a lack of it, blocks progress. Problems with balance and proportion, an agreement, the law, or one or more of its many agents may interfere. Dishonesty, vengeance, or even being too fair and honest are all to be avoided. Do not volunteer information.

YOUR FOUNDATION

4

Crucial to your situation is how truthful you have been with yourself and others. Records, paperwork and agreements must be put in order before further work is done. A knowledge of the law is vital.

WHAT IS BEHIND YOU

5

In the past, justice was done and the truth was revealed, whether or not anyone noticed or agreed. A deal from the past requires attention now. The influence of laws and lawyers is waning, though never far away.

WHAT CROWNS YOU

6

It would be good to purify yourself of vengeful feelings or regret. Visualize yourself forgiving all you feel have wronged you, including yourself for allowing it to happen. Realize that truth really is beauty and beauty, truth.

WHAT IS BEFORE YOU

7

You will soon get what you deserve. Agreements may be made and upheld. There may be a rebalancing on all levels, including financial and legal matters. Truth and justice will prevail. Your life will be beautified in some way.

YOUR PERSONA

8

Present yourself as fair, impartial and devoted to seeking the truth, not just for your own benefit. Show that you are willing to compromise as long as it is fair to all concerned. Dress as well as you can comfortably afford.

How Others See You

The wise see you as fair, impartial, devoted to finding truth and justice, and as one who may compromise if all are treated fairly. The ignorant may think you are a "straight arrow." You are seen by many as having good taste and judgement.

Your Hopes and Fears

You hope truth and justice will triumph but fear that it would do so in its own way and not yours. What you deserve might not be what you would like. You may fear lawyers or that a legal matter will go against you.

The Outcome

You will get what you deserve. Agreements may be made and upheld. There may be a rebalancing on all levels including financial and legal matters. Truth and justice will prevail. Your life will be beautified in some way.

Suspension

12 ◇ The Hanged Man

12 ◆ The Hanged Man:

Suspension

1

YOU

You need to get in touch with why you feel restricted or stuck. The suspension of progress may occur if learning reaches a plateau. If things are seen from a new perspective, change can occur. You are not being punished unjustly.

2

WHAT SURROUNDS YOU

You are surrounded by a feeling of suspension and forces that seem to want to restrict your every move. Try not be a martyr. Only when you can look at things from a different perspective will you suddenly feel free.

3

WHAT BLOCKS YOU

Suspension blocks progress. An enforced suspension of the usual way of doing things or too much freedom limits you. You cannot go forward or backward until you learn to look at things from a totally different perspective.

YOUR FOUNDATION

Crucial to your situation is your ability to see the value of limitation, of waiting and of the status quo. If you learn from this you may prosper. If you struggle, you will lose. Suspend your ordinary beliefs for a time.

WHAT IS BEHIND YOU

You are coming out of a time when you felt restricted or even martyred. The normal rules of doing things seemed suspended. You may have had to sacrifice for a higher purpose. Your new point of view will serve you well.

WHAT CROWNS YOU

It would be good to learn the value in ordinary life and in things staying as they are for now. Visualize yourself suspended over your situation and gaining a higher perspective. Know your new point of view can free you.

WHAT IS BEFORE YOU

You will soon come to feel like you are in suspended animation. This is a sign you must look at things from a different perspective or see the value in hanging in there for awhile. Know you are not being unjustly punished.

YOUR PERSONA

Present yourself as someone who must wait and cannot move from where you are physically, mentally or spiritually. Show you are ready to sacrifice for a worthy cause. Suspend yourself between action and inaction.

How Others See You

Others see you as being unable to move. Some see you trapped by your own thoughts and deeds while others see you as bound by forces over which you have little control. You may seem to be up in the air about something.

Your Hopes and Fears

You hope to take the time out of your everyday life to look at things from a different perspective, but fear you will still feel restricted no matter what you do, say or think. You may fear being suspended or trapped. You may fear heights.

The Outcome

You may come to feel you are in suspended animation. It is a sign you must see things from a different and higher perspective. Make the most of delays beyond your control. Know you are not being unjustly punished.

Transformation

13 ◇ Death

⬧13⬧ Death:

Trans- formation

YOU

You need to profoundly transform yourself or a situation. If you cannot transform the situation, you must be willing to let it go. What has outlived its time must pass away to make way for new growth.

WHAT SURROUNDS YOU

You are surrounded by energies that require and support profound change. They may be painful if resisted. What has outlived its time is being cleared away to make way for new growth. An agreement may end.

WHAT BLOCKS YOU

Too much or too little transformation is blocking progress. Too much causes pain and confusion and can cost you dearly. Too little transformation inhibits growth. The fear of death or profound change is also in the way.

YOUR FOUNDATION

4

Crucial to your situation is your attitude towards and experience with transformation. You cannot resist it or count on things to stay the same. Better to let go and let God/dess. You must "clean house" and make way for the new.

WHAT IS BEHIND YOU

5

You are coming out of a period of profound transformation. Change can be painful, especially if it is resisted. If this was the case, let the pain go so you can move forward. If you failed to "clean house," it may haunt you.

WHAT CROWNS YOU

6

It would be good to let go of fear and allow transformation to take place. Visualize yourself in a garden in fall as flowers fade and plants drop their seeds. Feel the sun cause the seeds to burst forth with new life in the spring.

WHAT IS BEFORE YOU

7

You will soon cope with profound transformation. You may have to end something or let it go to make room for something new. Resisting change can be painful so let go and let God/dess. One cycle will end so another can begin.

YOUR PERSONA

8

Present yourself as an agent of change. Show that you know we must let go to make way for the new when the old has outlived its time. Seek closure. Show you are ready to close the deal or kill it. It is time to "clean house."

How Others See You

Others see you as an agent of profound change. You seem able to let go to make way for the new when the old has outlived its time. You appear to seek closure. You can "clean house," close a deal or kill it.

Your Hopes and Fears

You hope the transformation your life must go through will not cause you unbearable pain, but fear it will. You are stronger than that. It is too much or too little fear of death or profound change that should, itself, be feared.

The Outcome

You may have to cope with profound transformation. You may have to let something go to make room for something new. Resisting change can be painful so let go and let God/dess. It will be time to "clean house."

Patience

14 ◇ Temperance

14 Temperance:

Patience

1

YOU

You need to be patient so that you can act with timing and precision. Test yourself: do you feel anxious or in harmony with practical considerations and natural laws? Learn how to mix, blend, stir and wait.

2

WHAT SURROUNDS YOU

The energies around you call for patience and attention to the timing of your actions. It is a time for moderation. Keep mixing, blending and stirring. It may be better to let things come to you.

3

WHAT BLOCKS YOU

Problems with patience and timing block progress. Too much patience delays attainment of your goal and can result in ignorance being tolerated. Not enough patience also destroys timing and hurts all involved.

Your Foundation

Crucial to your situation is your ability to be patient and productively use time spent waiting. Preparation allows you to act most effectively and with good timing. Make lists. Prioritize. Set reasonable goals and meet them.

What is Behind You

The time of patience, mixing and waiting has passed. If this time was used well, all is prepared for effective action. If time was wasted, stop complaining. You must stop, look and listen before you act.

What Crowns You

It would be good to have the patience necessary to plan and act with good timing. Visualize yourself being instructed in the art of patience by your Guardian Angel. Know that you must enjoy the process as much as the result.

What is Before You

You will soon encounter a time when patience, punctuality or acting with precise timing will determine your success. Use waiting time wisely so you are prepared to act. Complexity may benefit you so do not reject it.

Your Persona

Present yourself as moderate in all things—patient, punctual and able to act with precise timing. Show you can successfully blend seemingly opposing factors to work for you. Display your skill at mixing, blending and stirring.

How Others See You

9

Others value your ability to be moderate in all things, your patience, punctuality and precise timing. Those with an inflexible agenda may see you as overly pragmatic, vacillating or using delaying tactics.

Your Hopes and Fears

10

You hope you can be patient enough to act with the precise timing necessary to optimize your effectiveness, but you fear that circumstances require that you act now. You may fear diluting your purity or strength.

The Outcome

11

You will come to see the wisdom in waiting. Being patient, punctual or acting with precise timing may determine your success. Consideration will pay rich dividends. Complexity may benefit you, so do not reject it out of hand.

Trickery

15 The Devil: Trickery

YOU

1

You think you need something and you are willing to go against what you know to be right to obtain it. You are playing a risky game with dangerous forces. Trickery will backfire. Sex without love is meaningless.

WHAT SURROUNDS YOU

2

You are surrounded by trickery and temptations. Beware. Someone may be lying to you. Choose your words carefully. Do not volunteer information. It is a time of seduction and ulterior motives. Play the game to win.

WHAT BLOCKS YOU

3

Trickery, dishonesty and temptation blocks progress. Protect yourself. Someone may be lying to you. It may be you who is lying to others or even yourself. Lust or lack of love, caring and empathy ensures eventual failure. Act subtly or not at all.

4 YOUR FOUNDATION

Crucial to the situation is your ability to wear a mask and play the game, always remembering that it is only a game. Beware of seduction, theft, lies and trickery by others or yourself. Act subtly or do not act at all.

5 WHAT IS BEHIND YOU

The seduction of the material world is lessening its grip on the present situation. The influence of lust, selfishness, trickery and even criminal activity must be considered in your present situation. Act with subtlety.

6 WHAT CROWNS YOU

It would be good to put on the act necessary to deal with trickery. Visualize yourself wearing a protective mask given to you by your Guardian Angel. Remember to take it off when you are through playing the game.

7 WHAT IS BEFORE YOU

Beware. You will soon be faced with the seduction of the material world. You may be tempted and tested by lust, trickery and greed. You may have to mask your real intentions. Act with subtlety or do not act at all.

8 YOUR PERSONA

Present yourself as someone who knows how to play the game to win. Be subtle and careful not to reveal too much. Mask even that, for if you seem too capable of trickery you may not be trusted by anyone. Act sexy or seductively.

HOW OTHERS SEE YOU

Others do not see you as you are. Many see you as seductive and tempting. Some think you are capable of bending the truth to your purpose. A few think you are capable of evil. Do not expect to be supported by others.

YOUR HOPES AND FEARS

You hope to possess pleasures of the material world but fear attaining it means dealing with the worst in people, including yourself. Our shadow-side must always be dealt with. You may fear sex and other temptations or the purgatory described by some religions.

THE OUTCOME

Beware. You will be faced with the seduction of the material world. You may be tempted and tested by lust, trickery and greed. You may have to mask your real intentions. Act with subtlety or do not act at all.

16 The Tower

Crisis

16 The Tower:

Crisis

YOU

You need to revolutionize an important aspect of your situation. You may feel so desperate that you are willing to upset everything and everyone to end your crisis. Volatile or nervous energy may be released suddenly.

WHAT SURROUNDS YOU

You are surrounded by revolutionary ideas and actions. The status quo must change or a crisis may occur. Stability is threatened. Pressure must be released or an "explosion" may occur. Energy will be released suddenly.

WHAT BLOCKS YOU

Crisis and instability blocks your progress. Forces of change or the resistance to change have caused a breakdown. If the old has been swept aside, much good has been lost with it. Balance must be restored.

4 YOUR FOUNDATION

Crucial to your situation is your ability to function well in an unstable, crisis-ridden time when everything changes rapidly. The Chinese characters for "crisis" are "danger" and "opportunity." Be alert to them both.

5 WHAT IS BEHIND YOU

Passing is a time of instability, revolutionary ideas and the breakdown of established structures. The effects of this time are indelible and must be faced and understood. The opportunity to re-create your life is now.

6 WHAT CROWNS YOU

It would be good to escape the pressures of your life by doing something in an entirely new way. Visualize yourself happily re-inventing your life, throwing out what has not worked for you in the past.

7 WHAT IS BEFORE YOU

You will soon encounter revolutionary ideas, instability or the breakdown of established structures. Volatile energies may be released quite suddenly. The old rules will no longer apply. You may be liberated in some way.

8 YOUR PERSONA

Present yourself as a champion of exciting, revolutionary, new and innovative ideas. Show the benefits of updating established ideas and structures to new realities. Do not be shy or fear rocking the boat.

HOW OTHERS SEE YOU

Progressives see you as a champion of what is exciting and revolutionary. You seem unafraid of change. Conservatives see you as a wild, dangerous or disruptive influence trying to destroy what they treasure most in life.

YOUR HOPES AND FEARS

You may wish to see established patterns and structures revolutionized and the routine made exciting, but fear the instability and disruption will not be worth the effort. You may fear disaster will strike.

THE OUTCOME

You will encounter revolutionary ideas, instability or the breakdown of established structures. Volatile energies may be released quite suddenly. The old rules will no longer apply. You may be liberated in some way.

17 ◇ The Star

Illumination

The Star:

Illuminatio

YOU

You need to be the star of your "show" and experience a time of joy, wonder, hope and healing. Relax and re-establish your connection with your body and the illumination of spiritual realities. Dwell on the good.

WHAT SURROUNDS YOU

You are surrounded by wondrous possibilities: joy, hope, healing and maybe even fame. Beauty, art and spiritual truths can inspire refreshingly new ideas that transcend "reality." It is a time of renewal and illumination.

WHAT BLOCKS YOU

Idealism blocks progress. Do not use the search for beauty, art, spiritual truth, joy, wonder, hope or healing as a way to avoid reality. The distasteful has its place in life. Balance relaxation with satisfying work.

YOUR FOUNDATION

Crucial to your situation is having the time and the ability to heal and rejuvenate. Use beauty, art and spiritual truths to inspire hope, joy and illumination. For now, avoid the distasteful. Be a "star" in your own show.

WHAT IS BEHIND YOU

The time for healing, relaxing and re-energizing is passing. The inspiration, hope and sense of wonder gained can empower faith. Spiritual truths can make dreams come true. The benefits of illumination endure.

WHAT CROWNS YOU

It would be good to heal and re-energize. Surround yourself with art, beauty and only positive things. Visualize these powerful, positive energies pouring out of all these things to heal, empower and illuminate your life.

WHAT IS BEFORE YOU

You will soon know the benefits and the necessity of relaxation, healing and rejuvenation. You may experience divine grace and spiritual illumination. Enjoy being the "star" of your show. Know that you need and deserve a time for healing after the storm.

YOUR PERSONA

Present yourself as an agent for peace, healing, hope and inspiration. Avoid negativity. Show the value of illumination, and of expressing and appreciating art and beauty. Be relaxed. You may even act like a "star."

HOW OTHERS SEE YOU

Others see you as an agent for peace, healing, hope and inspiration. They bask in your glow. Your enjoyment of spiritual truths illuminates the darkness in their lives. Some think you have "star" quality.

YOUR HOPES AND FEARS

You hope you will be able to heal and rejuvenate, but fear you will not. You may think it naive to focus on the positive and ignore the limiting effects of focusing on the negative. You may fear the rigors of seeking illumination.

THE OUTCOME

You will know the benefits and the necessity of relaxation, healing and rejuvenation. You may know divine grace and spiritual illumination. Enjoy being the "star" of your show. Know that you need and deserve a time for healing after the storm.

18 ◇ The Moon

Night Journey

◆ 18 **The Moon:**

Night Journey

1 | YOU

You need to go on without a clear picture of where you are, where you are going or where you have been. You do not have to fear the unknown. With intuition and faith in yourself and benevolent forces you can succeed.

2 | WHAT SURROUNDS YOU

You are surrounded by darkness that makes it hard to separate illusion from reality. The path may seem frightening. Trust your intuition. Do not go by experts, fashion and rumor. Act as if benevolent forces are with you.

3 | WHAT BLOCKS YOU

You may be paralyzed by darkness, fear or confusion. To separate illusion from reality may be impossible or impractical. With intuition and faith in yourself and benevolent forces you can make your journey through the unknown.

Your Foundation

4 Crucial to your situation is your ability to go on without knowing exactly where you stand. The path may seem frightening, but stay calm and have faith that your intuition and benevolent forces will lead you safely home.

What is Behind You

5 A time of darkness, fear and confusion is passing. Its profound effect may not be entirely apparent. If faith, trust and intuition are still valuable to you, you are now the better for it. If not, get the nurturing of a real friend.

What Crowns You

6 It would be good to believe you can navigate through this time of darkness, fear or confusion. Visualize the fact that even on a cloudy night the moon is beyond the clouds trying to push back darkness and show you the way.

What is Before You

7 You may soon encounter darkness, fear or confusion. You will be challenged to go on without a clear picture of the past, present or future. Depend on faith, intuition and benevolent forces to lead you safely home. Get in touch with your dreams.

Your Persona

8 Present yourself as on a journey from darkness to the light, from fear to faith, and from confusion to clarity. You may be moody. You may be lonely or frightened. This is a time of testing, a proverbial "dark night of the soul."

How Others See You

Others see you as moody. To those who only see the surface of things, you may seem lonely, frightened or confused. The wise and the experienced see you are finding your way through a proverbial "dark night of the soul."

Your Hopes and Fears

You hope the fear and confusion will end, but you fear strength, faith and trust in divine protection is not enough. Divine forces speak to us through dreams and intuition. You may fear the unknown, strangers or the dark.

The Outcome

You may encounter darkness, fear or confusion. You will be challenged to go on without a clear picture of the past, present or future. Depend on faith, intuition and benevolent forces to lead you safely home. Get in touch with your dreams.

19 ◆ The Sun

Radiance

19 The Sun:

Radiance

1

YOU

You need to share your highest qualities and achievements. Radiate who you are and what you are doing always and all ways. Shine love on those you care about. Be a strong, paternal figure. Support all efforts to grow.

2

WHAT SURROUNDS YOU

You are surrounded by strong positive energies. Everything looks sunny and bright. What was hidden is revealed. Creativity is expressed and recognized. Love is freely given. There is love, light and laughter available.

3

WHAT BLOCKS YOU

Being too optimistic or pessimistic blocks your progress. Focusing on publicity, gifts or giving obscures real issues. Too much or too little input from friends or family can cause problems. Things cannot always be good.

Your Foundation

Crucial to your situation is your ability to radiate love, warmth and kindness. Emulate the Sun's life-giving creative ability. Support all efforts to grow. Share the story of your achievements and good fortune with all.

What is Behind You

You are coming out of a time and place of love, warmth, gift-giving and grace. Feel the memory of it envelope you. Let your successes empower you; don't dwell on your failures. You have a good foundation to build upon.

What Crowns You

It would be good to enjoy and radiate love, warmth and creative energy. Visualize yourself as the Sun giving light that makes life possible. Feel that light penetrating you and your life, destroying darkness and ignorance.

What is Before You

You will soon enter a period where everything looks sunny and bright. Love, friendships or a patron's gift may empower you or your creativity. Family will be more important than ever. You may go to a warm climate.

Your Persona

Present yourself as a champion of those trying to grow. Radiate love, warmth and good cheer upon all you meet. Be a shining example of the best you are capable of becoming. Show optimism, no matter what.

How Others See You

Others see you as possessed of a sunny disposition. They value your energy, creativity and your ability to radiate love and warmth. You seem to support efforts to grow. Cynics see you as overly optimistic and proud.

Your Hopes and Fears

You hope everything will be sunny and bright, like in a children's book, but fear this is too much to expect. Ideals are goals. To live in paradise you must realize that it is the enjoyment of the process of attaining goals that is important.

The Outcome

You will enter a period where everything looks sunny and bright. Love, friendships or a patron's gift may empower you or your creativity. Family will be more important than ever. You may go to a warm or sunny climate.

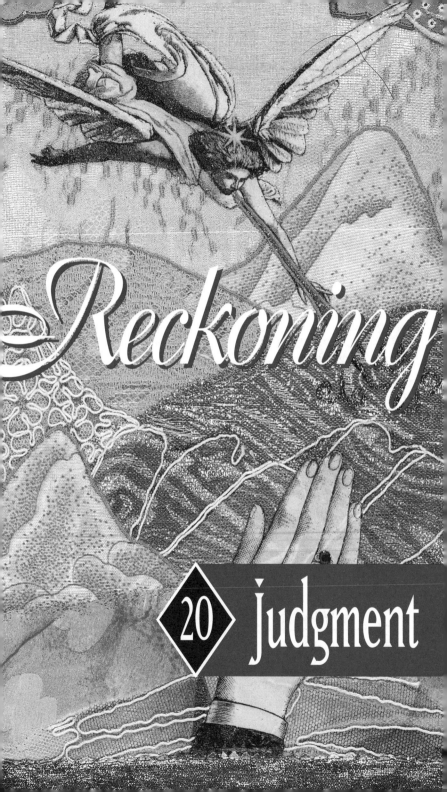

Reckoning

 Judgement:

Reckoning

 1

YOU

You need to evaluate past actions to become more aware of who you are and of your ultimate goals. This reckoning may surprise and may lead to endings, beginnings and the resurrection of things once thought dead or resolved.

 2

WHAT SURROUNDS YOU

You are compelled to evaluate past actions, become more aware of what is real and of ultimate goals. Surprising revelations may lead to beginnings, endings and the resurrection of things once thought dead or resolved.

 3

WHAT BLOCKS YOU

Damage caused by the misuse of criticism or the refusal to awaken to what is real can block progress. You may be judged and found wanting if you ignore the voice of your Higher Self and fail to prepare for a time of reckoning.

YOUR FOUNDATION

4 Crucial to your situation is your ability to exercise good judgment. Poor decision-making causes most suffering. An oracle can help you develop this skill. Evaluate past actions, strengths and limits. Keep good records.

WHAT IS BEHIND YOU

5 The influence of a time of reckoning is passing. This settling of accounts may have produced surprising revelations which led to beginnings, endings and the resurrection of things once thought dead or resolved.

WHAT CROWNS YOU

6 It would be good to make a conscious effort to settle accounts and balance past karma. Visualize an angelic herald reminding all that a time of reckoning and judgment is near and atonement will be required.

WHAT IS BEFORE YOU

7 You will soon enter a time of reckoning and judgment. Prepare for accounts to be settled and past karma to be balanced. Surprising revelations may cause beginnings, endings and the resurrection of things from the past.

YOUR PERSONA

8 Present yourself as a master of the art of decision-making. Make sure your Higher Self guides your judgment. Seek to settle accounts and balance all past karma. An oracle can help you develop your decision-making skills.

How Others See You

Others see you as desirous of settling accounts and balancing past karma. Most think you are guided by your Higher Self. Others think ego is the motivation for your judgments. Some think you are a prophet of doom.

Your Hopes and Fears

You hope you can settle accounts and balance past karma, but fear there may not be the will or resources to do so. You would like to resurrect what passed away before its time, but fear the consequences of even trying.

The Outcome

You will enter a time of reckoning and judgment. Prepare for accounts to be settled and past karma to be balanced. Surprising revelations may cause beginnings, endings or the resurrection of things thought dead or resolved.

Culmination

21 The World

21 The World:

Culminatio

YOU

You need to attain a degree of understanding that enables you to graduate to a higher level and enjoy real success. This rare time of culmination must be identified and honored. As the old cycle ends, inappropriate habits must be left behind.

WHAT SURROUNDS YOU

You are surrounded by the possibility of knowing the best the world has to offer. Hard work pays off now. Now is the time to gain advancement. A major cycle ends as a new one begins. Seize this moment of culmination.

WHAT BLOCKS YOU

The completion, or incompletion, of a major cycle blocks progress. There are problems with graduation. Old or inappropriate habits may interfere. Do not get too far ahead of yourself. Culmination causes new challenges.

YOUR FOUNDATION

Crucial to your situation is your awareness of the cyclical nature of existence and the desire to move onward and upward. Graduation to succeeding levels is required to transcend limits. Savor the moment of culmination.

WHAT IS BEHIND YOU

A major cycle has been completed and a new level has been reached. Like the eternal seasons, this culmination reminds us of our eternal connection to the world. Expect a time of new rules, methods and challenges to deal with.

WHAT CROWNS YOU

It would be good to take things to a level more appropriate with the new realities of your life. Visualize the world evolving, divinely guided by the same forces that guide your evolution. See the culmination of life's plan.

WHAT IS BEFORE YOU

You will soon attain a degree of achievement and understanding that enables you to graduate to a higher level and enjoy physical, mental and spiritual rewards. Savor this time of culmination. You have earned it.

YOUR PERSONA

Present yourself as completing a major stage in your evolution. Show that after you have graduated and savored this time of culmination, you look forward to the next cycle. Be more aware of long-range and global matters. Act worldly.

How Others See You

Others see you as having attained a degree of achievement and wisdom that enables you to enjoy the gifts of the world on the physical, mental and spiritual levels. You seem worldly and aware of long-range and global matters.

Your Hopes and Fears

You hope to attain a degree of achievement and wisdom that enables you to graduate to a higher level, but fear you will not be able to transcend where you are now. You may fear to leave your corner of the world.

The Outcome

You will soon attain a degree of achievement and understanding that enables you to graduate to a higher level and enjoy rewards of a physical, mental and spiritual nature. Savor this time of culmination. You have earned it.

Initiation

♦ Ace of Wands:

Initiation

1

You

You need to be instinctive, creative and passionate. You are being initiated. Do not second-guess yourself. Go on first impressions. Make the first move. Try to see through all illusion. You may experience a breakthrough.

2

What Surrounds You

You are surrounded by passion and creative energy. A fiery animal magnetism around you burns away darkness, enabling you to see how to initiate action. A breakthrough may be occurring. A test needs to be passed.

3

What Blocks You

You may be too impulsive and aggressive about a new passion. Or, you may lack the energy it takes to begin a new project. Try not to burn out. You may see through a deception that was meant to protect you. A test or initiation period may not be over or may cause trouble.

YOUR FOUNDATION

Crucial to your situation is having the vitality and enthusiasm to initiate a new project. Make the first move. Focus your energy and break through every barrier. See through illusion. Do not second guess yourself. Pass the test.

WHAT IS BEHIND YOU

In the past, a new opportunity arose for taking action. If action was instinctively initiated without any second guesses, all is well. If not, act carefully and only if you are sure of what excites you. It may be hard to break through resistance or sustain your passion now.

WHAT CROWNS YOU

It would be good to pass the test and be able to initiate a new project. Visualize yourself as a phoenix rising from the ashes in a burst of glory and power. Nothing can hold you back as you break through all illusions.

WHAT IS BEFORE YOU

You will soon be involved in the initiation of a new and exciting project. Be passionate, spontaneous and creative. Make the first move. Go by first impressions. This is a time of tests, new beginnings, initiation and breakthrough.

YOUR PERSONA

Present yourself as an aggressive, passionate, energetic and creative person who seeks to break though all limits. Initiate a new project. Do not hesitate or second-guess yourself. Make it clear that others must pass your test.

HOW OTHERS SEE YOU

Others see you as a fiery, enthusiastic, energetic and creative person who seeks to break through all limitation. Some think you are vivacious and a strong motivational force. Rigid types see you as testy, impulsive and aggressive.

YOUR HOPES AND FEARS

You hope to leap to a new level of passion and vital growth and feel ready, willing and able to do so, but you fear you are being too impulsive. You may lose out if you do not act immediately. You fear you may not pass the test.

THE OUTCOME

You will be involved in the initiation of a new and exciting project. Be passionate, spontaneous and creative. Make the first move. Go by first impressions. This is a time of testing new beginnings, initiation and breakthrough.

◈ Two of Wands

Planning

Two of Wands:

Planning

1 YOU

You need to pause and contemplate where you are, where you have been and where you are going. You are at a crossroads. Make a plan before you take any action. You are in a position of power and can take time out to do so.

2 WHAT SURROUNDS YOU

You are surrounded by the need to plan for growth, renewal and independence. This is a time to map out broad plans before you are forced to return to taking care of the details. Things are at a crossroads now.

3 WHAT BLOCKS YOU

Planning, or a lack of it, blocks progress. Taking too much time to deliberate or having too many plans and directions to explore is as counterproductive as doing no planning at all. You are at a crossroads.

YOUR FOUNDATION

Crucial to your situation is taking time out to assess the present and plan for the future. Free from distractions, map out broad plans and foresee how to take care of all the details. You are at a crossroads.

WHAT IS BEHIND YOU

In the past, you reached a crossroads and had the chance to assess your situation and plan for the future. If you did so, you should now be in a position to make good decisions. If not, you may have to plan on the run.

WHAT CROWNS YOU

It would be good to take some quiet time for mapping out your plan. Visualize yourself on a cloud overlooking your situation. See the big picture of how things are. See what is coming down the road toward you.

WHAT IS BEFORE YOU

You will soon reach a crossroads. You will look back over where you have come from and look forward to where you want to go. You will start to map out a strong plan to explore many new directions and may become established, independent and ready to expand.

YOUR PERSONA

Present yourself as calm, deliberate and ready to assert yourself if needed. Act as if you are established and independent and can take the time to map out a strong plan. Show you are at a crossroads and have several choices.

How Others See You

Others see you as established and independent, in a position of decision-making power. They see you as master of all you survey—strong, balanced and confident in your plans. Some think you are at a crucial crossroads.

Your Hopes and Fears

You hope you can take some time out to rest, review your goals and make new plans, but fear you will have to work out the details before you are ready. You may fear that your ability to plan or your sense of direction is poor.

The Outcome

You will reach a crossroads. You will look back over where you have come from and where you want to go. You will start to map out a strong plan to explore many new directions and may become established, independent and ready to expand.

Opportunity

♦ Three of Wands

Three of Wands:

Opportunity

YOU

You need to become more aware of opportunities that exist for you right now. There may be more than you are aware of. To best see and take advantage of them you must concentrate, cooperate and remain open-minded.

WHAT SURROUNDS YOU

You are surrounded by opportunities, both obvious and hidden. Do not expect them to come in any pre-conceived time, place or form. Look at everything as if for the first time and you will see them. It is time to advance yourself.

WHAT BLOCKS YOU

Opportunities, or a lack of them, block progress. If there are too many, you must chose the one that speaks equally to your head and heart. It there are too few, you must create your own luck. You may be missing an opportunity right in front of you. Look for it.

Your Foundation

Crucial to your situation is the ability to cooperate and concentrate while staying open to opportunity in whatever time, place or form it comes. This is the time to sow the seeds of success. Use all of your resources.

What is Behind You

In the past, opportunities came to you in many ways. If you were open to them, you profited. If you refused to see those that came in unusual forms, you wasted time. Be open-minded now and you will not miss out again.

What Crowns You

It would be good to see and use all the opportunities around you. Visualize your situation as a child would, seeing it for the first time. Assume nothing. Question everything and everyone. A beginner's mind is an expert's tool.

What is Before You

You will soon become aware of at least one great opportunity. It may not come in the form you expect. If you are alert, open-minded and willing to cooperate, you will get your wish. The time to meet a great playmate, and maybe even your soul-mate, may be drawing near.

Your Persona

Present yourself as an opportunity waiting to be properly exploited. Show you are creative, inventive and open-minded. Blend child-like openness with practicality and cooperation. Show you could make a great friend and maybe even more.

HOW OTHERS SEE YOU

Others see you as an opportunity waiting to be properly exploited. You seem creative, inventive and open-minded. You blend child-like openness with practicality and cooperation. You seem like you would make a good friend or maybe even more.

YOUR HOPES AND FEARS

You hope that a new and exciting opportunity will come into your life and work out well, but fear it might not happen. Embrace the unknown. It is where opportunities come from. You may fear, or fear for, a friend.

THE OUTCOME

You will become aware of at least one great opportunity. It may not come in the form you expect. If you are alert, open-minded and willing to cooperate, you will get your wish. The time to meet a great playmate, and maybe even your soul-mate, may be here.

Completion

Four of Wands

◆ Four of Wands:

Completion

1

YOU

You need to ceremoniously acknowledge and celebrate the completion of an important course of action. Give thanks for the support, friendship and good things in your life. Enjoy mutual support with another. Feel complete.

2

WHAT SURROUNDS YOU

You are surrounded by harmony and support. Proven partners provide benefit. There is a feeling of celebration, achievement and optimism. You are surrounded by the kind of happiness that must be shared to be known.

3

WHAT BLOCKS YOU

A deal must be closed before you celebrate. Focus too much on the end and you ignore the process. Failure to complete or commit shows fear of judgment or of getting on with life. Old relationship problems may re-surface.

YOUR FOUNDATION

Crucial to the situation is your commitment to bring things to completion. Be supportive and nurture harmonious relationships. Be optimistic and grateful. Make a strong foundation. Stay with proven partners.

WHAT IS BEHIND YOU

In the past, you saw the results of being committed and bringing things to completion. If you avoided obligations, you wasted time. Nurture harmonious relationships now and you will benefit in the future.

WHAT CROWNS YOU

It would be good to celebrate and give thanks for your good fortune. Visualize a rainbow and a bluebird singing a song of thankfulness to the world, a reward for a job well done. Partake of the world's sweetness.

WHAT IS BEFORE YOU

You will soon enjoy satisfaction from the completion of an important course of action. Your hard work will pay off. Proven partners will come through. Appropriate tokens of appreciation can be exchanged to honor what has been achieved. An important date is coming up soon.

YOUR PERSONA

Present yourself as a thankful, tranquil and secure person, one who is able to close a deal, fulfill obligations and otherwise bring things to completion. Show you are learning how to have a mutually supportive relationship.

How Others See You

Others see you as a thankful, tranquil and secure person who is able to close a deal, fulfill obligations and otherwise bring things to completion. They see you are learning how to have a mutually supportive relationship.

Your Hopes and Fears

You hope your labors have created a strong foundation, one you can finally celebrate, but fear you are being too optimistic. You may fear commitment and closure. Or, you may be afraid of the process of growing old with a special someone.

The Outcome

You will enjoy satisfaction from the completion of an important course of action. Your hard work will pay off. Proven partners will come through. Appropriate tokens of appreciation can be exchanged to honor what has been achieved. An important date is coming up.

Competition

◆ Five of Wands

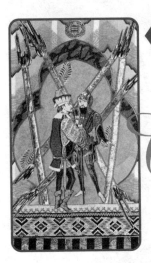

◆ Five of Wands:

Competition

1 YOU

You need to experience what competition really means and requires. Respect your opponent but stand up for your point of view. Refuse to be a victim. Fight the tendency toward frustration, anger, hate and prejudice.

2 WHAT SURROUNDS YOU

You are surrounded by an air of competitiveness, frustration and anger. It can hurt you or strengthen your resolve to stand up for yourself. Fight the tendency toward prejudice and hate or they will hurt you, too.

3 WHAT BLOCKS YOU

Being too competitive or not competitive enough can block you. Anger and frustration can prevent you from acting effectively. Recognize hate and prejudice in yourself and in others and eliminate them. Respect your opponent.

4 YOUR FOUNDATION

Crucial to your situation is your ability to compete while respecting your opponent. Even though you are angry and frustrated, never let hate, fear or prejudice destroy your reason. Competition is a tool for self-improvement.

5 WHAT IS BEHIND YOU

In the past, you saw the results of competition. If frustration was allowed to turn into hate, anger and prejudice, time was wasted. Eliminate the desire for revenge. Respect your opponent now and you will benefit.

6 WHAT CROWNS YOU

It would be good to be competitive while respecting your opponent. Visualize yourself in your opponents situation and see how it would be possible to take that point of view. See how your position looks from there.

7 WHAT IS BEFORE YOU

You will soon experience what competition really means and requires. Respect your opponent but stand up for your point of view. Refuse to be a victim. Fight against frustration, anger, hate and prejudice or they will hurt you, too.

8 YOUR PERSONA

Present yourself as a worthy opponent who knows to show respect for the other side while standing up for your point of view. Show you realize you must fight against frustration, anger, hate and prejudice or suffer them.

How Others See You

Others see you as the competition. You seem unwilling to concede defeat or even compromise. Some think you quarrelsome, prejudiced, frustrated or hateful. Even if this is not true, you still cannot convince them to see things your way.

Your Hopes and Fears

You hope you can compete head-to-head and win, but fear you may not be able to. Do not allow fear to turn to anger and prejudice. Winning by deceit will cost you more in the end. You may fear or fear for a competitor.

The Outcome

You will experience what competition really means and requires. Respect your opponent but stand up for your point of view. Refuse to be a victim. Fight against frustration, anger, hate and prejudice or they will hurt you, too.

Victory

Six of Wands

♦ Six of Wands:

Victory

1 YOU

You need to know what victory really means and requires. You know how to win, but it will last longer if you really want what you are going for. Share your success with your supporters and position yourself for the next challenge.

2 WHAT SURROUNDS YOU

You are surrounded by conditions favoring victory. Your victory is real, but it will last longer if you really want what you have strived for. Share your success with your supporters and position yourself for the next challenge.

3 WHAT BLOCKS YOU

Victory, or a lack of it, blocks progress. Focus on winning and you ignore your game. Victory is fleeting. Do not let loss stop you. Make sure you want what you are fighting for. You have not won yet.

YOUR FOUNDATION

4

Crucial to your situation is your ability to use victory to your advantage. It will last longer if it is shared with all who made it happen. They can then help you prepare for future challenges. Be certain you want what you strive for.

WHAT IS BEHIND YOU

5

In the past, you saw the results of being victorious. If you acted like victory would last forever, time was wasted. If you shared your success and made friends and allies, you are well positioned now to enjoy another victory.

WHAT CROWNS YOU

6

It would be good to ensure your eventual victory. Visualize yourself as having already won. Feel how victory feels to you. Adjust your attitude, if necessary. Make plans to solidify gains and prepare for future challenges.

WHAT IS BEFORE YOU

7

You will soon know what victory really means and requires. You may finally win. Your win will last longer if it is shared with all who made it happen. They can then help you prepare for future challenges. The spotlight will be on you.

YOUR PERSONA

8

Present yourself as one who has won victory and knows why. Recognize those who can help you meet the next challenge. Celebrate your victory. Show that, though you know how fleeting it is, you can do it again.

HOW OTHERS SEE YOU

Others see you as one who has won victory and knows why. They know you appreciate those who have helped you and can help with future challenges. Everyone loves a winner. They want to help you celebrate.

YOUR HOPES AND FEARS

You hope that you will attain victory, but you fear you may not. Or, you may fear the changes in your life that victory will bring. You may fear to admit that victory, like life itself, is fleeting, for that may stop your hot pursuit.

THE OUTCOME

You will know what victory really means and requires. You may finally win. Your win will last longer if it is shared with all who made it happen. They can then help you prepare for future challenges. The spotlight will be on you.

Courage

Seven of Wands

Seven of Wands:

Courage

1

YOU

You need to know what courage really means. Go forward in spite of your fears. Defend the things you love. Do not compromise your position. You may need to go it alone. Come out from behind your defenses and act.

2

WHAT SURROUNDS YOU

You are surrounded by an air of courage and bravery. What is valuable is being defended. Positions will not be given up without a fight. There is a willingness to go it alone, if need be. Go forward in spite of your fears.

3

WHAT BLOCKS YOU

Courage, or a lack of it, blocks your progress. You may be overestimating a threat to you and what you love. Or, you may not know that bravery means going forward in spite of fear. You may be defensive without reason.

YOUR FOUNDATION

4

Crucial to your situation is courage. It is vital to go forward in spite of your fears. Defend the things you love. Do not compromise your position. You may need to go it alone. Come out from behind your defenses and act.

WHAT IS BEHIND YOU

5

In the past, you saw what it takes to show true courage. If you let fear stop you from going forward, time was wasted. The lessons of that time can help you if you apply them now. Break down defenses with trust and love.

WHAT CROWNS YOU

6

It would be good to display real courage. Visualize yourself in front of your fortress wall taking on all comers. Feel yourself draw invincible strength from the rightness of your cause. See your attackers fall before you.

WHAT IS BEFORE YOU

7

You will soon know what courage means and requires. You will go forward in spite of your fears and defend without compromise the things you hold dear. You may have to be willing to go it alone, if need be. Assert yourself.

YOUR PERSONA

8

Present yourself as one who knows what courage means. Go forward in spite of fear. Defend what must be defended. Do not compromise your position. You must be willing to go it alone, if need be. Assert yourself.

How Others See You

Others see you as courageous. They know you will go forward in spite of your fears, defend the things you hold dear without compromising and will go it alone, if need be. Those uncomfortable with aggression dislike you.

Your Hopes and Fears

You hope you can display true courage, but fear you may not be able to go on despite your fears. You may fear that aggression or defending yourself is not spiritual. Learn why martial arts can be a high form of spiritual practice.

The Outcome

You will know what courage means and requires. You will go forward in spite of your fears and defend the things you hold dear without compromising. You may have to be willing to go it alone, if need be. Assert yourself.

Eight of Wands

Signals

Eight of Wands:

Signals

1

You

You need to make your intentions perfectly clear before taking action. Plans, directions and messages of love, romance and appreciation must be communicated and understood. Do it and do it now. Do not waste time.

2

What Surrounds You

You are surrounded by signs and symbols that are signaling what is going on around you. You must use your senses, logic and intuition to know what is truly being communicated. Do it and do it now. Do not waste time.

3

What Blocks You

Communication problems block progress. Pay close attention. Revealing too much or too little is as bad as revealing it too soon or too late. Failure to make intentions, romantic and otherwise, perfectly clear wastes time. Make sure signals do not get crossed.

4 YOUR FOUNDATION

Crucial to your situation is making sure intentions are clear and understood before action is taken. All concerned must know how much they are appreciated or loved. Keep the stream of communications flowing.

5 WHAT IS BEHIND YOU

In the past, intentions should have been clearly communicated and understood before action was taken. If not, time was wasted. Apply the lessons of that time to this situation. Keep communications flowing now.

6 WHAT CROWNS YOU

It would be good if intentions were clearly communicated and understood before action was taken. Visualize a light connecting your heart to the heart you need to reach. See both hearts pulsing in sync.

7 WHAT IS BEFORE YOU

You will soon make sure all intentions, both romantic and otherwise, are perfectly clear. Plans and directions, as well as messages of love, romance and appreciation will be exchanged. Communications will be kept flowing.

8 YOUR PERSONA

Present yourself as someone who knows how important it is for all intentions, romantic and otherwise, to be communicated and understood before action is taken. Become adept at a new method of communicating. Keep the lines of communication open.

How Others See You

Others see you as someone who knows how important it is for all intentions, romantic and otherwise, to be communicated and understood before action is taken. The taciturn might think you talk a little too much.

Your Hopes and Fears

You hope that all intentions, romantic and otherwise, will be understood and communicated, but fear it might not happen. You may be afraid to express your love and appreciation. You may fear a communications breakdown.

The Outcome

You will make sure all intentions, both romantic and otherwise, are perfectly clear. Plans and directions, as well as messages of love, romance and appreciation will be exchanged. Communications will be kept flowing.

Nine of Wands

Discipline

Nine of Wands:

Discipline

1

YOU

You need to be disciplined. The strength of your will, character and body may soon be tested. Gather and preserve your resources now so you may confidently defend your position later. Stay faithful to your purpose.

2

WHAT SURROUNDS YOU

You are surrounded by an air of discipline and self-confidence. There is much strength in reserve, but pleasure may be postponed. A position must be defended at all costs. Staying faithful to a purpose is vital.

3

WHAT BLOCKS YOU

Discipline, or a lack of it, blocks progress. Being too discipliined—denying real needs or being too rigid—can cause problems. Being overly self-indulgent and undisciplined also wastes time. Stay faithful to your cause, but only if it is a worthy one.

YOUR FOUNDATION

Crucial to your situation is being disciplined and developing strength of character, will and body. Resources must be preserved so your position can be defended with confidence. Stay faithful to your purpose.

WHAT IS BEHIND YOU

In the past, discipline and self-denial should have been used to develop strength of will, character and body. If not, time was wasted. Apply the lessons of that time to this situation. The influence of that time is waning.

WHAT CROWNS YOU

It would be good to be disciplined enough to do what you know must be done. Visualize yourself in the military and being given a direct order you have no choice but to obey. Realize you have the power to give that order and to obey it.

WHAT IS BEFORE YOU

You will soon evaluate the wisdom of being disciplined. You may postpone short-term pleasures for long-term goals. You may see a reason to defend and preserve your position and resources. You will stay faithful to your present cause.

YOUR PERSONA

Present yourself as a strong and disciplined person willing to postpone short-term pleasures for long-term goals. Demonstrate that you know how to be faithful. Defend and preserve your position and resources.

HOW OTHERS SEE YOU

Others see you as a strong, faithful and disciplined person willing to postpone short-term pleasures for long-term goals. Most know you will defend and preserve your position or resources. Some think you too rigid.

YOUR HOPES AND FEARS

You hope you can be disciplined enough to do what must be done, but fear you may not be able to. You may fear that being disciplined will require you to postpone pleasures. It will. You may fear having to obey an order.

THE OUTCOME

You will evaluate the wisdom of being disciplined. You may postpone short-term pleasures for long-term goals. You may see a reason to defend and preserve your position and resources. You will stay faithful to your present cause.

Ten of Wands

Oppression

Ten of Wands:

Oppression

You

You need to stop working so hard. If you cannot stop, then conserve your energy and pace yourself. When you are over-committed everything becomes a strain. Delay making decisions if exhaustion prevents good judgment.

What Surrounds You

You are surrounded by forces of oppression which require more of you than you can give. Though stressed and over-committed, you must go on, doing what you must do, not what you want. Conserve your energy and pace yourself.

What Blocks You

Oppressive forces block progress. Stress, overwork and over-commitment can drain you and cause you to make bad decisions. Conserve energy and pace yourself. Doing what you feel you must do, without motivation, wastes time. Make your decisions when you are not exhausted.

YOUR FOUNDATION

Crucial to the situation is your ability to keep going even though you are stressed, exhausted and over-committed. Goals must be clearly defined so not a drop of energy is wasted. Conserve your energy and pace yourself.

WHAT IS BEHIND YOU

In the past, you saw the results of stress, overwork and oppressive conditions. You may have been so drained that you could not make any plans. Take the time to renew your energy and spirit now and you will benefit greatly.

WHAT CROWNS YOU

It would be good to cope with stress, overwork, over-commitment and oppressive conditions. Visualize yourself drawing pure energy from the universe to get you through this time. Realize you cannot do what you want right now.

WHAT IS BEFORE YOU

You will soon encounter oppressive conditions. Overwork, stress and over-commitment may drain you and prevent clear thinking. Conserve energy, pace yourself, define goals clearly and do what you must to get through.

YOUR PERSONA

Present yourself as having a lot of irons in the fire. Show you are so stressed, overworked and over-committed that you barely have enough energy and resources to get you through this time. You cannot make decisions or take on anything new now.

How Others See You

Others see you as having a lot of irons in the fire. They know you are so stressed, overworked and over-committed that you barely have enough energy and resources to get you through this time. You clearly cannot make any decisions right now.

Your Hopes and Fears

You hope one or more of your many irons in the fire will pay off, but fear you will be overwhelmed by your commitments if they do pay off or even if they do not. You may be afraid of oppressive forces restricting your freedom.

The Outcome

You will encounter oppressive conditions. Overwork, stress and over-commitment may drain you and prevent clear thinking. Conserve energy, pace yourself, define goals clearly and do what you must to get through.

Princess of Wands

Impulsiveness

Princess of Wands

Impulsiveness

1

YOU

You need to be positive and spontaneous, not impulsive. Your enthusiasm impresses others but impatience and being quick to anger or lose interest can cost you and waste time. Your actions speak louder than your words.

2

WHAT SURROUNDS YOU

You are surrounded by spontaneity and enthusiasm which may turn to impatience, anger and theatrics if control is lost. News of an opportunity is near. A blunt, fiery or impulsive person may help or need help.

3

WHAT BLOCKS YOU

Impulsiveness blocks your progress. Impatience or hasty, immature actions may waste time. Lack of spontaneity and enthusiasm is also limiting. A blunt, fiery or impulsive person may be the problem.

YOUR FOUNDATION

Crucial to your situation is your ability to be spontaneous and enthusiastic while guarding against anger, impatience, impulsiveness, fickleness and other signs of immaturity. Dealing with the bluntness of a young person is vital.

WHAT IS BEHIND YOU

In the past, you saw how impatience and rash, impulsive acts can turn spontaneity and enthusiasm into fickleness and tactlessness. Apply those lessons now. The influence of an impulsive person may be waning.

WHAT CROWNS YOU

It would be good to be spontaneous and enthusiastic without being impulsive or fickle. Visualize yourself at a party to promote yourself and your cause, socializing but keeping your goal in mind as you do so.

WHAT IS BEFORE YOU

You will soon encounter or have to act like a person who is spontaneous and enthusiastic. Be careful that impulsiveness does not turn into tactlessness, anger and immature theatrics. If control of the situation is lost, stay calm.

YOUR PERSONA

Present yourself as spontaneous, enthusiastic and ready to respond immediately to any situation. Bring energy to all you do, though you may have to be blunt to do so. You may have to appear impatient, impulsive or younger than you are.

HOW OTHERS SEE YOU

Others see you as youthful, spontaneous, enthusiastic and ready to respond quickly to anything. Most think you bring energy to all you do. A few see you as tactless, immature, impulsive and fickle, unable to finish what you start.

YOUR HOPES AND FEARS

You hope to be spontaneous and enthusiastic, but fear that you seem impulsive, impatient or immature. You may fear losing your inhibitions or your youthfulness. You may fear, or fear for, an impulsive person.

THE OUTCOME

You will encounter or have to act like a person who is spontaneous and enthusiastic. Be careful that impulsiveness does not turn into tactlessness, anger and immature theatrics. If control of the situation is lost, stay calm.

Prince of Wands

Ambition

Prince of Wands:

Ambition

1

YOU

You need to move from where you are now to where you know you should be to increase your effectiveness in the world. There is nothing wrong with ambition. Be a pioneer. Take calculated risks. Do not brag, just do it.

2

WHAT SURROUNDS YOU

You are surrounded by ambition. The motivation to advance is strong. Favors must be exchanged or there will be quarrels, especially if authority is questioned. An ambitious person may help or need help.

3

WHAT BLOCKS YOU

Ambition, or a lack of it, blocks your progress. Too much ambition can cause real opportunities to be missed. Lack of ambition also wastes time. Moving may cause problems. Or, an ambitious person may be the problem.

YOUR FOUNDATION

Crucial to your situation is your ability to function well while on the move or without a stable home base. Use contacts to their full advantage. Avoid quarrels and do not brag. Dealing with the ambitions of a young person is vital.

WHAT IS BEHIND YOU

In the past, you saw ego and ambition both motivate and cause problems. Moves made then affect the current situation, for good or ill. Move carefully now. An ambitious person's influence may be waning.

WHAT CROWNS YOU

It would be good to have your ambitions become your reality. Visualize yourself living life the way you would like to. See what you will see when you have attained your dream and feel how you will feel. Hold those thoughts and feelings wherever you go.

WHAT IS BEFORE YOU

You will soon encounter or have to act like an ambitious person on the move. You may change your residence or position. Moving can incite irritability and quarrels. Stay calm. A passionate, pioneering spirit may take you far.

YOUR PERSONA

Present yourself as an ambitious person who desires to move to the best place possible. Show you are acting boldly to be first in your field and you are willing to take calculated risks. Do not be afraid to be passionate.

How Others See You

Others see you as an ambitious person. You appear to be on the move. You seem passionate and willing to take calculated risks. Some see you unable to put down roots. A few see you as an overbearing, quarrelsome showoff.

Your Hopes and Fears

You hope to fulfill your ambitions, but fear the drastic changes that would occur in your life. You may fear what moving from where you are now would bring. You may fear, or fear for, an ambitious person.

The Outcome

You will encounter or have to act like an ambitious person on the move. You may change your residence or position. Moving can incite irritability and quarrels. Stay calm. A passionate, pioneering spirit may take you far.

Inspiration

◆ Queen of Wands

Queen of Wands:

Inspiration

1 YOU

You need to feel inspired. Be a charismatic, self-assured person who knows how things must be done. Behave like royalty. Parties and other gatherings will benefit you. Find a creative project that fully occupies you. Inspire others.

2 WHAT SURROUNDS YOU

You are surrounded by an air of charisma and self-assurance. There is no lack of direction or directors. Business and finances are favored. Loyalty and energy abound. An inspiring person may help or need help.

3 WHAT BLOCKS YOU

Inspiration, or a lack of it, can block progress. Inspiration without hard work accomplishes nothing. Lack of inspiration is boring and also wastes time. An inspiring, charismatic person may be the cause of your trouble.

YOUR FOUNDATION

4

Crucial to your situation is your ability to be inspired and inspiring. A charismatic, self-assured person can best implement a vitally important project. Dealing with the inspiration of a group of people is vital. Play no favorites.

WHAT IS BEHIND YOU

5

In the past, you saw the benefits and drawbacks of being inspired. If your inspiration went unrealized or provoked hostility, time was wasted. Apply the lessons of that time now. The inspiration of the past is waning.

WHAT CROWNS YOU

6

It would be good to be both inspired and inspiring. Visualize yourself as an integral part of the majesty of Life. Feel the inspiring energy of the universe flowing through you. If you feel goose-bumps, you are plugged in.

WHAT IS BEFORE YOU

7

You will soon encounter or have to act like a charismatic, self-assured person who knows how things must be done. You may come across a situation, cause or creative project that inspires you to act. You may inspire others.

YOUR PERSONA

8

Present yourself as a charismatic, self-assured person who knows how things must be done. Show that you are loyal, have excellent business skills and your energy level is steady. Attend and enjoy social gatherings. Be an inspiration.

How Others See You

9

Others see you as an inspiring, vigorous person who knows how life works and how to get things done. You can sometimes seem a bit bossy but loyal and skilled in business. You seem always ready to support a worthy cause.

Your Hopes and Fears

10

You hope you can be inspired and inspire others, but fear you may not be able to. You may fear your temper will work against you. You may fear parties. You may fear, or fear for,an inspiring, charismatic person or for someone you depend on.

The Outcome

11

You will encounter or have to act like a charismatic, self-assured person who knows how things must be done. You may come across a situation, cause or creative project that inspires you to act. You may inspire others.

Dynamism

King of Wands

king of Wands:

Dynamism

1

YOU

You need to act dynamically to get your way. Confront your strengths and weaknesses. Once they are clearly seen, you can use this self-knowledge to your advantage. A truly scientific, mathematical approach will work best.

2

WHAT SURROUNDS YOU

You are surrounded by dynamic forces acting relentlessly to get their way. Power and pride are key issues. Be aware that strengths and weaknesses will be assessed and exploited. A dynamic person may help or need help.

3

WHAT BLOCKS YOU

The dynamics of the situation—strengths, weaknesses and other forces—block progress. Use them, along with science and math, correctly and you will win. Watch the bottom line. A dynamic or overbearing person may be the problem.

Your Foundation

Crucial to your situation is your ability to take dynamic action to accomplish goals. Strengths and weaknesses must be identified and exploited. A scientific, mathematical approach is best. Dealing with the energy of a dynamic person is vital.

What is Behind You

The dynamics of the past affect the present situation. The power, strengths and weaknesses of all involved need to be re-assessed and re-structured. A dynamic person's influence, though once strong, may now be waning.

What Crowns You

It would be good to act dynamically to accomplish your goals. Visualize yourself as the King of Wands: a fiery, self-confident ruler who, like his symbol the Sun, explodes into action, shining light and warmth on all.

What is Before You

You will soon encounter or have to act as a dynamic, dominant person who is absolutely sure she or he is right. Decisive action will be taken. Loyalty will be rewarded. Meanness, pettiness and cheapness will be punished.

Your Persona

Present yourself as a dynamic, dominant person who is absolutely sure you are right. Show neither doubt nor fear. Reward loyalty. Punish those who deserve it. Take on all situations that present themselves to you.

How Others See You

Others see you as a dynamic, dominant person who is absolutely sure you are right. You show neither doubt nor fear. You appear ready to reward the righteous and punish the unjust. Some see you as an arrogant gambler.

Your Hopes and Fears

You hope to act dynamically and without doubt to identify and exploit the strengths and weaknesses of all concerned, but fear you may fail. You may fear math or science. You may fear, or fear for, a dynamic person or for someone who is leading you in some way.

The Outcome

You will encounter or have to act as a dynamic, dominant person who is absolutely sure she or he is right. Decisive action will be taken. Loyalty will be rewarded. Meanness, pettiness and cheapness will be punished.

Triumph

◆Ace of Swords:
Triumph

YOU

You need to identify the long-term goals and major principles that will enable you to make your life a statement of your unique personality. Open up a channel to sacred wisdom. Triumph over adversity and ignorance.

WHAT SURROUNDS YOU

You are surrounded by forces trying to triumph over adversity and ignorance. A brilliant idea, setting long-term goals and standing up for major principles can help you make your mark. A channel is opening up. Cut away all "dead wood."

WHAT BLOCKS YOU

Forcefulness can block progress. Denying that failure may occur hampers any planning for it. Trying to be too pushy will not work. Too few or too many new ideas, long-term goals and major principles may be hindering you.

YOUR FOUNDATION

Crucial to your situation is your ability to triumph over adversity and ignorance. Long-term goals and major principles can enable you to cut through lies and illusion and open up a channel to sacred wisdom.

WHAT IS BEHIND YOU

The triumphs of the past, or the belief there were none, affects the present situation. Forcing things does not work over time. Long term goals and major principles help cut through illusions and open a channel to wisdom.

WHAT CROWNS YOU

It would be good to triumph over adversity and ignorance. Visualize yourself holding the sword depicted in the Ace of Swords. Realize that its two edges can be used to cut through illusion and defend major principles.

WHAT IS BEFORE YOU

You will soon triumph over lies, adversity and ignorance. A brilliant new idea, long-term goal or major principle will reveal itself. Your life's unique purpose will become more clear. A channel to sacred wisdom will open.

YOUR PERSONA

Present yourself as a someone working to triumph over adversity and ignorance. Forcefully cut through lies and illusions and get to the heart of the matter. Be the embodiment of your life's goals and highest principles.

How Others See You

Others see you as working to triumph over adversity and ignorance. They see you have no patience with deception of any kind and always cut to the heart of the matter. They know your ideas and words will destroy what no longer works.

Your Hopes and Fears

You hope you can triumph over adversity and ignorance, but fear you may not have the strength to do so. You may fear the results of destroying lies and illusions, or of being too forceful. You may believe that it is "not nice" to assert yourself.

The Outcome

You will triumph over lies, adversity and ignorance. A brilliant new idea, a long-term goal or a major principle will reveal itself. Your life's unique purpose will become more clear. A channel to sacred wisdom will open.

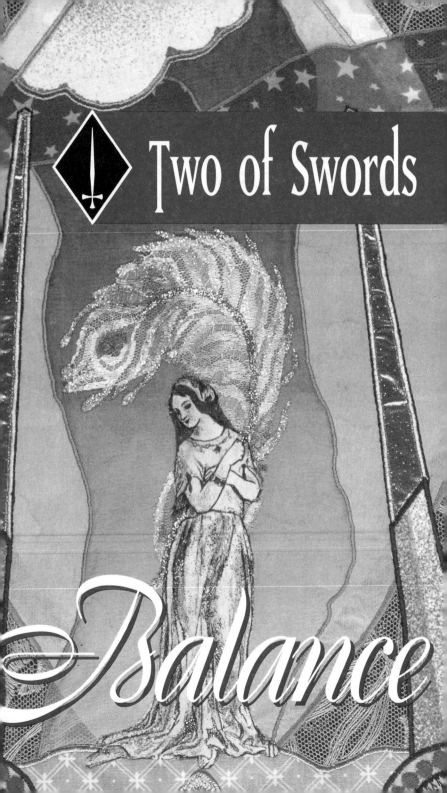

Two of Swords

Balance

Two of Swords:

Balance

1

YOU

You need to take a break from your usual way of thinking, seeing and doing to consider alternative ideas and viewpoints. Rest and relaxation are important now. Be diplomatic. Compromise or let things stand as they are.

2

WHAT SURROUNDS YOU

You are surrounded by an air of balance, diplomacy and compromise. A rest or break from usual ways of thinking, seeing and doing is called for. To avoid procrastination, or a stalemate, all viewpoints must be included.

3

WHAT BLOCKS YOU

Taking time out, or failing to, can block progress. Compromise can turn into surrender and sacrifice. Lack of balance brings powerful forces seeking to restore it. A break may have turned into procrastination or stalemate. Be sure to get enough rest.

YOUR FOUNDATION

Crucial to your situation is taking a break from usual ways of thinking, seeing and doing to rest or consider alternative ideas and viewpoints. Diplomacy and compromise can help achieve balance and harmony.

WHAT IS BEHIND YOU

The past achievement of balance, or the lack of it, affects the present situation. It was important that a break be taken from the usual way of thinking, seeing and doing. Compromise and diplomacy were needed.

WHAT CROWNS YOU

It would be good to achieve balance in all things. Visualize yourself easily walking a tightrope without fear, thoroughly enjoying yourself. Know you can achieve balance by valuing moderation, contentment and harmony.

WHAT IS BEFORE YOU

You will soon take a break from usual ways of thinking, seeing and doing to rest and consider alternative ideas and viewpoints. Diplomacy and compromise will achieve balance and avoid procrastination and stalemate. Take a vacation.

YOUR PERSONA

Present yourself as taking a break from usual ways of thinking, seeing and doing to consider alternative ideas and viewpoints. Show diplomacy and a willingness to compromise. Seek balance and harmony. Get enough rest.

How Others See You

Others see you as taking a break from usual ways of thinking and doing to consider alternative ideas and viewpoints. You seem diplomatic and ready to compromise. Some may see you as timid, lazy or as a procrastinator.

Your Hopes and Fears

You hope you can achieve balance and harmony, but fear you may not be able to. You may fear that you are giving up more than you gain. Or, you may fear that compromise may be mistaken for weakness.

The Outcome

You will take a break from usual ways of thinking, seeing and doing to rest and consider alternative ideas and viewpoints. Diplomacy and compromise will achieve balance and avoid procrastination and stalemate. Take a vacation.

Three of Swords

Sorrow

Three of Swords:

Sorrow

YOU

1

You need to get in touch with pain and sorrow. Denying that they exist leads to loss, hostility and dis-ease. Though life seems meaningless, recovery can occur. It takes faith, self-love, forgiveness and time. Count your blessings.

WHAT SURROUNDS YOU

2

You are surrounded by the potential to know pain and sorrow. Denying it can lead to loss, hostility and dis-ease. Protect yourself. Defenses are weak and must be strengthened. Do not let the problems of another affect you.

WHAT BLOCKS YOU

3

Sorrow blocks progress. Though life may seem meaningless, do not deny the pain is real. Healing and recovery takes faith, forgiveness, self-love, and time. Count your blessings. Peace begins when expectations end.

Your Foundation

Crucial to your situation is your ability to know sorrow and pain without sinking into despair and surrender. Sorrow is healed by love, faith, learning from what has happened and forgiving yourself and others.

What is Behind You

Past sorrow and pain is affecting the present situation. Find out how. If it was denied or repressed, it may have led to loss, hostility and dis-ease. If so, you must patiently promote healing with love and forgiveness.

What Crowns You

It would be good to recognize sorrow and pain and successfully deal with them. Visualize yourself as a spirit in flesh whose true purpose is as a soul traveling onward, growing through knowledge born of earthly experience.

What is Before You

You may soon encounter pain and sorrow in yourself or another. Your defenses may be weakened. Despair may engulf you. Count your blessings as you forgive yourself and others. Peace begins when expectations end.

Your Persona

Present yourself as someone experiencing pain and sorrow. You must work through the hurt, despair and bitter thoughts. Denying them would only lead to loss, hostility and dis-ease. Avoid self-pity and jealousy.

How Others See You

Others see you as experiencing loss, pain and sorrow. Your defenses appear to not be working. You may seem ill, hurt, jealous or sinking into the depths of despair. Some see you as wallowing in self-pity.

Your Hopes and Fears

You hope you can recognize and successfully cope with sorrow and pain, but fear you will not be able to overcome despair. Sorrow is healed by love, faith, learning from what has happened and forgiving yourself and others.

The Outcome

You may encounter pain and sorrow in either yourself or another. Your defenses may be weakened. Despair may engulf you. Count your blessings as you forgive yourself and others. Peace begins when expectations end.

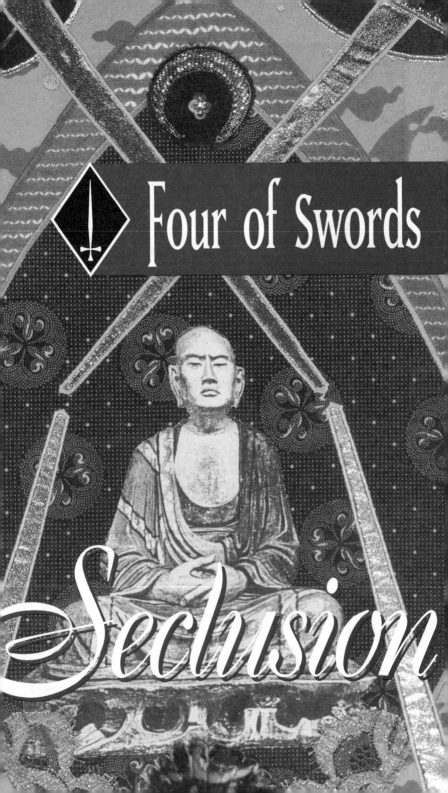

Four of Swords

Seclusion

Four of Swords:

Seclusion

1 ## YOU

You need seclusion to deal properly with your situation. Retreat from pain, conflict and distractions, and rid yourself of stress and anxiety. Ground and re-charge yourself. Look inward for a real change. Meditate daily. You can!

2 ## WHAT SURROUNDS YOU

You are surrounded by an air of calm detachment. Forces are pushing you into seclusion. Examine your thoughts without distractions or stress. It is time for strategic withdrawal. Take sanctuary wherever you find it.

3 ## WHAT BLOCKS YOU

Seclusion, or a lack of it, blocks progress. Isolation can prevent you from knowing what is really going on. Detachment may result in retreat when you should fight. Or, you may desperately need a break from stress and distraction.

Your Foundation

Crucial to your situation is your ability to recognize the value of seclusion, detachment and retreat as a method for accomplishing great things. To rid yourself of stress and anxiety, look inward for strength. Meditate daily. You can!

What is Behind You

The time of seclusion is passing. If the absence of distractions was used to gain inner strength, things will go well. If there was a retreat from issues that should have been faced, they will now have to be dealt with.

What Crowns You

It would be good to seclude yourself and meditate. Watch your breathing. When thoughts intrude, notice them as if from a distance and then watch them go. Do this ten minutes a day and you will become calm and focused.

What is Before You

You will soon evaluate seclusion, detachment and retreat as methods for accomplishing great things. You will avoid pain, conflict and distractions and lessen your stress and anxiety. Look inward to re-charge youself.

Your Persona

Present yourself as someone who knows the benefit of seclusion and retreat as methods for accomplishing great things. With calm detachment, look inward for solutions. Take a break from stress and strife. Meditate.

HOW OTHERS SEE YOU

Others see you as someone who knows the benefit of seclusion and retreat as methods for accomplishing great things. They see you are calm and detached and look inward for direction. Some think you are merely escaping.

YOUR HOPES AND FEARS

You hope seclusion or detachment will help you rid yourself of stress, strife and distraction, but fear what calm and isolation may bring. You may fear other forms of spirituality or that you cannot meditate. You can!

THE OUTCOME

You will evaluate seclusion, detachment and retreat as methods for accomplishing great things. You will avoid pain, conflict and distractions and lessen your stress and anxiety. Looking inward will re-charge you.

Five of Swords

Defeat

Five of Swords:
Defeat

1 # You

You need to learn about surrender and defeat. The time of defeat is the best time to sow the seeds of future successes. You may have gotten what you wanted but it did not satisfy you. Be careful what you wish for.

2 # What Surrounds You

You are surrounded by an air of defeat. When the game is lost or victory's cost too high, accept it. Real defeat is in not learning from mistakes. Protect yourself from the defeats of others. Sew the seeds of future successes now.

3 # What Blocks You

Defeat blocks progress. A defeatist attitude guarantees loss. Know how to lose and know how to win. Do not be a sore loser or a sore winner. Learn from defeat. A hollow victory is draining. Someone you defeated may be the problem.

4 YOUR FOUNDATION

Crucial to your situation is your ability to deal with defeat and surrender. Defeat can work for you. The time of defeat is the best time to sow the seeds of future success. If you got what you wanted but it did not satisfy, learn from this.

5 WHAT IS BEHIND YOU

Past experiences dealing with surrender and defeat are affecting the present situation. If the lessons taught were ignored, it will probably happen again. You cannot cheat karma. Revenge or blame is unnecessary.

6 WHAT CROWNS YOU

It would be good to accept defeat as a lesson that can insure future success. Visualize your biggest defeat as someone else's problem. See what you can learn from it when you are removed from loss and gain.

7 WHAT IS BEFORE YOU

You may soon encounter defeat, either in your own situation or that of another. Or you may get what you want but find that it does not satisfy. The time of defeat is the best time to sow the seeds of future successes. Avoid blame and revenge.

8 YOUR PERSONA

Present yourself as someone who accepts defeat. Surrender can teach you a lesson that can insure future success, or it can be a pose to create a false sense of victory in others which you can exploit. Show you are disheartened.

9   HOW OTHERS SEE YOU

Others see you as defeated, weak and embittered. Many think you got what was coming to you. You seem vengeful and full of blame. Some think you are merely ignorant of or dissatisfied with the level of your success.

10   YOUR HOPES AND FEARS

You hope defeat will not destroy you, but fear that it will. You may not feel strong enough to learn from it and go on. You may fear revenge and blame. Or, you may think that you will be unhappy even if you win.

11   THE OUTCOME

You may encounter defeat, either in your own situation or that of another. Or, you may get what you want but find that it does not satisfy you. The time of defeat is the best time to sow the seeds of future successes. Avoid blame and revenge.

Passage

Six of Swords

Six of Swords:

Passage

1

YOU

You need to realize that you are now in a much better position in life. You endured a difficult transition and are now more able to deal with what may come. Change your beliefs about yourself. A trip will do you much good.

2

WHAT SURROUNDS YOU

You are surrounded by the forces of transition. A test, a trip or a rite of passage will lead to new beliefs and direction. You can move on to a new and better place in life. A foreign person may help or need help.

3

WHAT BLOCKS YOU

Travel blocks progress. Too much travel is as bad as too little. A trip may be delayed or not go as planned. A transition or change of direction may disappoint. To change your world, change your beliefs about it. A test may be failed.

4 YOUR FOUNDATION

Crucial to your situation is knowing how to pass from one state to another. This can mean traveling well, returning to your calm center after you have been disturbed, knowing how to camouflage, changing your beliefs, and more.

5 WHAT IS BEHIND YOU

A past test is affecting your present situation. If this rite of passage was not successfully navigated, you will feel the consequences now. A past trip, a change of direction or an important transition may also be affecting you.

6 WHAT CROWNS YOU

It would be good to view life's challenges as rites of passage which, when passed, admit you to ever higher levels of power and wisdom. Visualize the challenges in your life as doors which you can open to reveal rich rewards.

7 WHAT IS BEFORE YOU

You will soon see improvement. A test will be passed. Beliefs will change for the better. The ability to be calm and centered will increase. A positive transition will be made from one state to another. A trip will go very well.

8 YOUR PERSONA

Present yourself as going through a difficult rite of passage successfully and moving into a better time in your life. Show others how profound your transition is. Demonstrate how changing your beliefs changed your life.

How Others See You

Others see you as going through a difficult rite of passage successfully and moving into a better time in your life. Your transition appears to be profound. It seems that changing your beliefs has changed your life.

Your Hopes and Fears

You hope you can successfully navigate through a difficult rite of passage and move into a better time in your life, but fear you may not be able to. You may fear being tested. A trip may be causing you needless anxiety.

The Outcome

You will see improvement. A test will be passed. Beliefs will change for the better. The ability to be calm and centered will increase. A positive transition will be made from one state to another. A trip will go very well.

Opposition

Seven of Swords

Seven of Swords:

Opposition

1 YOU

You need to evaluate the opposition you are offering or encountering. Be logical, persistent and try not to respond in kind to deceit and trickery. See if any of your troubles are self-created. Eliminate your most negative behavior patterns.

2 WHAT SURROUNDS YOU

You are surrounded by opposition. You may not know the full extent of the opposing forces. Resources are being held in reserve. It will take a lot of effort to make things go your way. Reconsider your idea of what should be.

3 WHAT BLOCKS YOU

Opposition blocks progress. Things said and done behind others' backs, or manifestations of fears and prejudices may be the cause. No rash plan can prevent deceit from bringing you down. Use logic and subtlety.

YOUR FOUNDATION

Crucial to your situation is your ability to both offer and respond to opposition. Be logical, persistent and try not to resort to deception. Trouble is often self-created. Eliminate negative behavior patterns at once.

WHAT IS BEHIND YOU

Past opposition is affecting the present situation. Whether you opposed another or they you does not matter. What does is how the opposition was expressed, honestly or otherwise. Be aware of prejudice, fear and deceit.

WHAT CROWNS YOU

It would be good to deal correctly with opposition. Visualize yourself in the position of those who oppose you. See if they have a point or if they are merely selfish. If compromise is possible, do it. If not, plan carefully.

WHAT IS BEFORE YOU

You will soon evaluate the opposition you are encountering or creating. It may be very strong. With logic, persistence and self-examination, negative behavior patterns can be overcome. Be aware of prejudice, fear and deceit.

YOUR PERSONA

Present yourself as evaluating the strength and wisdom of the opposition you are encountering or creating. Show you know how much of it is self-created. Do not use any tricks you may have up your sleeve just yet. Keep them ready.

How Others See You

Others see you as evaluating the strength and wisdom of opposition you are encountering or creating. Many just see you as the opposition, ready to resort to anything to get what you want. You seem to be your own worst enemy.

Your Hopes and Fears

You hope you can overcome any opposition you encounter, but fear you may not be able to. You may fear having to resort to deceit to win. Or you may be afraid that you are your own worst enemy and cannot reform.

The Outcome

You will evaluate the opposition you are encountering or creating. It may be very strong. With logic, persistence and self-examination, negative behavior patterns can be overcome. Be aware of prejudice, fear and deceit. You may have to use all your reserves to win.

Eight of Swords

Indecision

Eight of Swords:

Indecision

1

YOU

You need to see the whole picture before you decide. In times of doubt and confusion, do not act immediately. Look patiently within for answers from your higher mind. No one else can decide for you. An oracle can help you.

2

WHAT SURROUNDS YOU

You are surrounded by indecision and inertia. Do not expect anything to happen soon. Rigidity, misunderstanding and focusing on petty details must be dealt with. Lack of perspective cripples faith. An oracle can help.

3

WHAT BLOCKS YOU

Indecision blocks progress. It can be yours or another's. Nothing is happening. Rigidity, misunderstanding and focusing on petty details must be dealt with. Lack of perspective cripples faith. An oracle can help you.

YOUR FOUNDATION

4

Crucial to your situation is your ability to deal with indecision. Sometimes you must decide not to decide. Rigidity, misunderstanding and focusing on petty details must be dealt with. An oracle can help you understand how you feel.

WHAT IS BEHIND YOU

5

Past indecision is affecting the present situation. It may be yours or that of another. If rigidity, misunderstanding and focusing on petty details were not dealt with then, they must be now. An oracle can help you now.

WHAT CROWNS YOU

6

It would be good to overcome indecision. Visualize yourself as the woman pictured on the Eight of Swords. Though seven swords hold you, realize you hold the sword of will power to cut yourself free—the eighth and most powerful one.

WHAT IS BEFORE YOU

7

You will soon encounter indecision in either yourself or another. There are times when it is best to decide not to decide. If a decision must be made, gather as much information as you can and let an oracle help you.

YOUR PERSONA

8

Present yourself as undecided. Show that you believe that sometimes it is best to decide not to decide. Try to see the whole picture. The regular use of a personal oracle can help you develop your decision-making ability.

How Others See You

Others see you have not made a definite decision. You may seem trapped by over-analyzation, unimportant details and the inability to see the whole picture. Some think you are an indecisive person. An oracle can help.

Your Hopes and Fears

You hope you can overcome indecision and inertia, but fear you may not be able to. You may fear that a bad decision may be worse than no decision at all. Remember sometimes it is best to decide not to decide. Consult an oracle.

The Outcome

You will encounter indecision in either yourself or another. There are times when it is best to decide not to decide. If a decision must be made, gather as much information as you can and let an oracle help you.

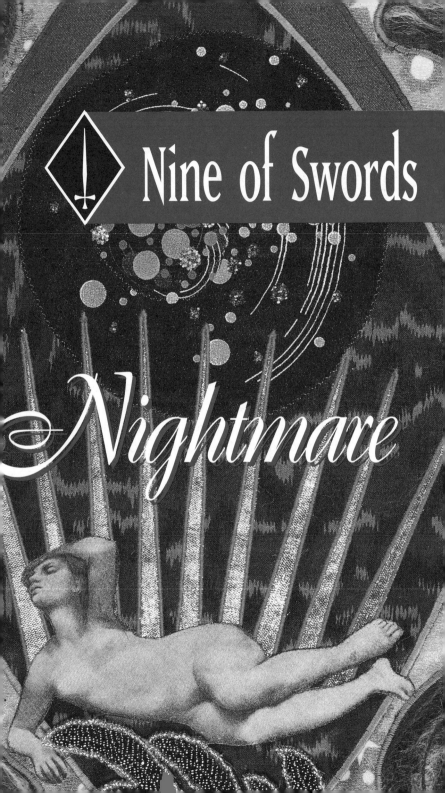

Nine of Swords

Nightmare

♦ Nine of Swords:

Nightmare

1

YOU

You need to realize that fears, if not confronted and understood, can lead to obsession, compulsion, paranoia or physical illness. We all have a dark side which must be acknowledged. Avoid being a martyr. Get enough sleep.

2

WHAT SURROUNDS YOU

You are surrounded by what seems a nightmarish situation. Fears, if not confronted and understood, can lead to obsession, compulsion, paranoia or physical illness. Protect yourself from negative forces. Get enough sleep.

3

WHAT BLOCKS YOU

A nightmarish situation blocks progress. Fears, if not confronted and understood, can lead to obsession, compulsion, paranoia or physical illness. Protect yourself from negative forces. Avoid being a martyr. Get enough sleep.

YOUR FOUNDATION

4 Crucial to your situation is your ability to deal with a nightmarish situation. Fears, if not confronted and understood, can lead to obsession, paranoia, compulsion or physical illness. Protect yourself from negative forces.

WHAT IS BEHIND YOU

5 Past fears, obsessions and compulsions are affecting the present situation. If they were confronted and understood, they will now manifest as bad memories, anxiety and nightmares. If not, take action today to do so.

WHAT CROWNS YOU

6 It would be good to deal well with fear, obsession and nightmares. As you go to sleep, visualize yourself safe in the arms of the one who loves you most. Ask how to deal with your problem. You will be answered.

WHAT IS BEFORE YOU

7 You may soon encounter, in yourself or another, a situation where fears must be confronted and understood or turn into obsession, compulsion, paranoia or physical illness. Avoid becoming a martyr. Get enough sleep.

YOUR PERSONA

8 Present yourself as in the grip of a nightmarish situation. Show you are in the process of confronting it and all fears so as to avoid becoming a martyr to obsession, compulsion, paranoia or physical illness. Get enough sleep.

How Others See You

Others see you in the grip of a nightmarish situation. Many see you as confronting it and all fears so as to avoid becoming a martyr to obsession, compulsion, paranoia or physical illness. Others fear to be with you.

Your Hopes and Fears

You hope you can deal with obsession, compulsion, paranoia or physical illness without becoming a martyr to them, but fear you may not be able to. Your dark side is a part of you. Accept it. You may fear being afraid. Learn how to deal with panic attacks.

The Outcome

You may encounter, in yourself or another, a situation where fears must be confronted and understood or they will turn into obsession, compulsion, paranoia, or physical illness. Avoid becoming a martyr. Get enough sleep.

Ten of Swords

Ruin

Ten of Swords:

Ruin

1 YOU

You need to know that the worst is over. Though the hopes and dreams of the past may be dashed, new ones will arise in time. If words cannot comfort, a wound this deep and loss this devastating may require professional help.

2 WHAT SURROUNDS YOU

You are surrounded by a ruinous situation. The worst may have happened. Though the hopes and dreams of the past may be dashed, new ones will arise in time. Professional help may be required to deal with wounds so deep.

3 WHAT BLOCKS YOU

Ruin blocks your progress. The worst may have happened. Though the hopes and dreams of the past may be gone, new ones will arise in time. Professional help may be required to deal with wounds so deep.

YOUR FOUNDATION

Crucial to your situation is your ability to cope with a ruinous situation. Though the hopes and dreams of the past may be gone, new ones will arise in time. Professional help may be required to deal with wounds so deep.

WHAT IS BEHIND YOU

A ruinous situation from the past is affecting the present situation. Though hopes and dreams were dashed, new ones should have arisen in time. If not, professional help may now be required to deal with such deep wounds.

WHAT CROWNS YOU

It would be good to know how to cope with ruin. Visualize yourself with someone who is much worse off than you and yet goes on. Their suffering and their example may inspire you, as yours may help another to go on.

WHAT IS BEFORE YOU

You may soon encounter a situation where the worst seems to have taken place, either to you or another. The hopes and dreams of the past may be gone. Professional help may be required to help you put your life in order.

YOUR PERSONA

Present yourself as realizing the worst has happened. You may realize that though the hopes and dreams of the past may be gone, new ones will come over time. If not, seek professional help to find new ones to replace the loss.

HOW OTHERS SEE YOU

Others see the worst has happened to you. Some think you know that though the hopes and dreams of the past may be gone, new ones will come over time. Others think you should seek a professional to help you recover.

YOUR HOPES AND FEARS

You hope you can cope with the ruin of your hopes and dreams, but fear you may not be able to. You may fear you have no reason to live. Realize that others are less fortunate. Or, you may fear seeking professional help.

THE OUTCOME

You may encounter a situation where the worst seems to have taken place, either to you or to another. The hopes and dreams of the past may be gone. Professional help may be required to help you put your life in order.

Princess of Swords

Ideas

Princess of Swords

Ideas

1

You

You need to appreciate and communicate ideas, information and theories. Abstract thinking can help you see weak spots in plans and systems. New information will produce surprises. Beware of gossip. Protect your privacy.

2

What Surrounds You

You are surrounded by the communication of information, ideas and theories. Abstract thinking and surprises expose weak spots in plans and systems. Protect privacy. A clever person may help or need help.

3

What Blocks You

Ideas, or a lack of them, block progress. Ideas without action are ineffective. Too few ideas or poor communication limits options and awareness. Expect surprises. Guard against scandal. A clever person may be the problem.

YOUR FOUNDATION

4 Crucial to your situation is your ability to appreciate and communicate information, ideas and theories. Abstract thinking and surprises can expose flaws in plans and systems. Dealing with the ideas of a young person is vital.

WHAT IS BEHIND YOU

5 Past ideas, information or gossip affect the present. If communication was clear, all is well. If not, plans and systems must be reevaluated now. Expect surprises. A clever person's influence may be waning.

WHAT CROWNS YOU

6 It would be good to appreciate and communicate ideas, information and theories. Visualize yourself placing ideas into sturdy boxes and sending them to others who open, understand them and send theirs back to you.

WHAT IS BEFORE YOU

7 You will soon encounter or have to act as a communicator of information, ideas and abstract theories. Some will be surprising. Your ability to be clear will be tested. Gossip, privacy, discretion and a young person may be involved.

YOUR PERSONA

8 Present yourself as a communicator of information, ideas and theories, some of them surprising. Show how abstract thinking can expose flaws in plans and systems. Learn and model the rules of gossip, privacy and discretion.

HOW OTHERS SEE YOU

Others see you as a communicator of information, ideas and theories, some of them surprising. Your ability to think abstractly exposes flaws in plans and systems. A few see you as a nosy gossip who is often indiscrete.

YOUR HOPES AND FEARS

You hope you communicate well, but fear you do not. Information, ideas, theories, and abstract thinking may frighten you. You may be fear gossip or indiscretion. Or, you may fear, or fear for a clever person.

THE OUTCOME

You will encounter or have to act as a communicator of information, ideas and abstract theories, some surprising. Your ability to be clear will be tested. Gossip, privacy, discretion and a young person may be involved.

Prince of Swords

Ingenuity

◆ Prince of Swords:

Ingenuity

YOU

You need to think of ways to turn ideas into reality. Develop your skills, ingenuity and self-esteem, or frustration and defensiveness will cause you trouble. Respond now with cleverness, outspokenness and foresight.

WHAT SURROUNDS YOU

You are surrounded by ingenuity. Ideas can be made real but frustrated plans may lead to aggression or defensiveness. Help is given only in return for equal favors. An outspoken person may help or need help.

WHAT BLOCKS YOU

Ingenuity, or a lack of it, blocks progress. You may be too clever for your own good. Plans may be elegant but impractical. Lack of ingenuity may cause aggressive behavior. An outspoken person may be the problem.

Your Foundation

4

Crucial to your situation is your ability to use your ingenuity as a response to frustrating challenges, not aggression or defensiveness. Cleverness turns ideas into reality. Dealing with the ingenuity of an outspoken young person is vital.

What is Behind You

5

The ingenuity of the past is affecting the present. Clever and farsighted ideas ensure success. Limited skills and shortsighted vision may have led to problems. The influence of an outspoken person may be waning.

What Crowns You

6

It would be good to develop your ingenuity. Visualize your current challenge and how you would solve it with unlimited resources. Then modify your solution in line with all resources available to you now.

What is Before You

7

You will soon encounter or act as an ingenious, clever and outspoken person who is not afraid to respond directly or fight for an idea. Be aware that frustrated plans or sarcastic words may cause defensiveness or aggression.

Your Persona

8

Present yourself as an ingenious, clever and outspoken person who is not afraid to respond directly or fight for an idea. Show you can turn ideas into reality with skill and foresight. Avoid sarcasm, frustration and aggression.

How Others See You

Others see you as ingenious, clever and outspoken, not afraid to respond directly or to fight for an idea. Most see you can turn ideas into reality with skill and foresight. Some think you are sarcastic, frustrated and too aggressive.

Your Hopes and Fears

You hope you can turn ideas into reality while staying true to your ideals, but fear you may not be able to. Frustration, defensiveness or aggression may concern you. You may fear, or fear for, an outspoken person.

The Outcome

You will encounter or act as an ingenious, clever and out-spoken person who is not afraid to respond directly or fight for an idea. Be aware that frustrated plans or sarcastic words may cause defensiveness or aggression.

Independence

Queen of Swords

Queen of Swords:

Independenc

1

YOU

You need to be independent. Empathy may distract you. Think with your head not with your heart. Devote your full attention and concentration to your situation or the volume of information will overwhelm. Tell it like it is.

2

WHAT SURROUNDS YOU

You are surrounded by energies that require and support independence. There is no room for sympathy. Ideas and information are powers being used and may be abused. A strong, independent person may help or need help.

3

WHAT BLOCKS YOU

Independence, or a lack of it, blocks progress. Acting unpredictably, or being disloyal or unmanageable destroys confidence and trust. The inability to function on your own also can waste time. A strong, independent person may be the problem.

Your Foundation

Crucial to your situation is your ability to think independently. Now, ideas and information are powers to be used wisely. There is no time for sympathy. Tell it like it is. A strong, direct and independent person may be important.

What is Behind You

Past ideas of independence affect the present situation. If information and ideas were seen as powers to be used, all is well. If not, use them now without regard for feelings. A strong, direct and independent person's influence may be waning.

What Crowns You

It would be good to think independently. Visualize yourself at the level of self-sufficiency you would like to achieve. How is it different from the way you live now? Use this information to see a way to make necessary changes.

What is Before You

You will soon encounter or have to act as an independent thinker who sees ideas and information as powers to be used. Sympathy will be lacking. Be careful loneliness does not turn strength into rigidity, tactlessness or prudishness.

Your Persona

Present yourself as a strong, independent person whose ideas and experiences determine your manner. Assert your right to go from frightening to frivolous and everywhere between. Avoid appearing bitter or prudish.

How Others See You

Others see you as a strong, independent person whose ideas and experiences define your manner, which fluctuates from frightening to frivolous. Some see you as lonely, hurt, cold, tactless, prudish or bitter.

Your Hopes and Fears

You hope you can be strong and independent, owing nothing, but fear you may not be able to. You may fear appearing lonely, cold, indifferent, prudish or bitter. You may fear, or fear for, a strong, independent person.

The Outcome

You will encounter or have to act as an independent thinker who sees ideas and information as powers to be used. Sympathy will be lacking. Be careful loneliness does not turn strength into rigidity, tactlessness or prudishness.

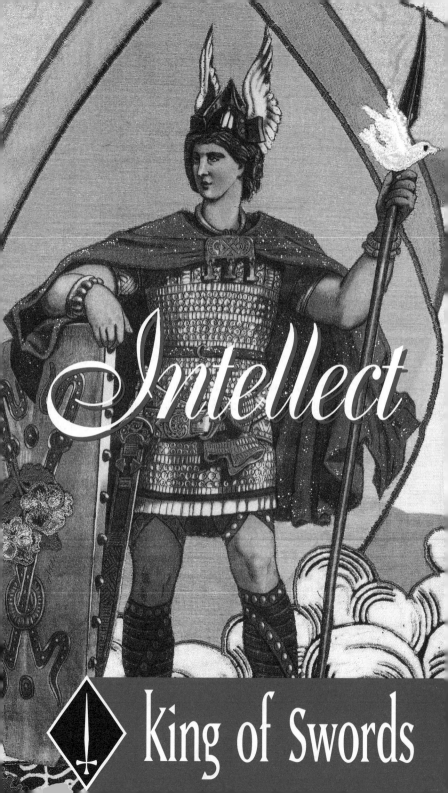

Intellect

King of Swords

King of Swords:

Intellect

1 | YOU

You need to use your intellect to get your way. Your schooling and knowledge of philosophy are important, but so are your idle thoughts and daydreams. You can also solve problems by using history, rules, laws and diplomacy.

2 | WHAT SURROUNDS YOU

You are surrounded by intellectual development, rules and history. Idle thoughts, brainstorming and daydreams are as vital as education and philosophy. A diplomatic, intellectual person may help or need help.

3 | WHAT BLOCKS YOU

Intellectualism, or a lack of it, blocks progress. Theories may fail when tested in practice. Intellectual development may be lacking or not valued enough. Diplomacy may also be a sore point. Or, an intellectual person may be the problem.

YOUR FOUNDATION

Crucial to your situation is intellectual development, rules and history. Idle thoughts, brainstorming and daydreams are as vital as education and philosophy. A diplomatic, intellectual person may be important.

WHAT IS BEHIND YOU

Past rules and intellectual development affect the present situation. If high-minded ideas were valued, all is well. If not, meanness must be overcome. A diplomatic, intellectual person's influence may be waning.

WHAT CROWNS YOU

It would be good to value the power of the intellect. Visualize yourself on a cloud looking down as the history of the world plays out beneath you. Realize all major changes were caused by ideas. Learn what they were.

WHAT IS BEFORE YOU

You will soon encounter or have to act as an intellectual person whose knowledge of history, rules, laws and diplomacy makes you very powerful. Schooling and the knowledge of philosophy will take on new importance.

YOUR PERSONA

Present yourself as an intellectual person whose knowledge of history, rules, laws and diplomacy makes you very powerful. Show schooling and philosophy are important. Demonstrate your ability to brainstorm well.

How Others See You

Others see you as an intellectual whose knowledge of history, rules, laws and diplomacy makes you powerful. Schooling, philosophy and the ability to brainstorm seem important to you. Some think you are off in the clouds.

Your Hopes and Fears

You hope you can use your intellect to get your way, but fear you may not. Schooling, philosophy, history, rules, laws, diplomacy or daydreams may concern you. You may fear, or fear for, a diplomatic, intellectual person.

The Outcome

You will encounter or have to act as an intellectual person whose knowledge of history, rules, laws and diplomacy makes you very powerful. Schooling and the knowledge of philosophy will take on new importance.

Ace of Hearts

Love

 **Ace of Hearts:**

Love

 1 # YOU

You need to experience the feeling of a new love or of giving and receiving unconditional love. Give and accept love on a new level. Open your heart and let emotions move you. Your loving ways will magnetize love to you.

 2 # WHAT SURROUNDS YOU

You are surrounded by love. The possibility to discover a new love affair is real. Open your heart to it. You can feel the most positive emotions. Loving ways will magnetize love to you. A lover may help or need help.

 3 # WHAT BLOCKS YOU

Love, or a lack of it, can block progress. Unconditional love is not always appropriate. Focusing on love affairs when work is to be done wastes time. Lack of love makes life seem meaningless. A lover may not really be good for you now.

Your Foundation

Crucial to your situation is your ability to give and receive unconditional love and know joy. Experience or recapture the feelings that arise in the early days of a real love affair. Dealing with the needs of a lover is vital.

What is Behind You

In the past, unconditional love or the feelings associated with a new love were felt. Love that endures is always maturing into something better. If not, it withers from stagnation. The influence of a past love may be waning.

What Crowns You

It would be good to know unconditional love or feel the heady excitement of a new love. Visualize your heart sprouting wings and flying skyward to join with the heart of one you love or of one who loves you. Draw love into you.

What is Before You

You will soon encounter or feel the heady excitement of a new love, even in an existing relationship. You may have the chance to experience the joy of giving and receiving with an open heart. Expect a pleasant surprise.

Your Persona

Present yourself as one who knows how to give and receive love unconditionally. Let the poignancy of life wash over you, cleansing your emotions and filling you with compassion. Everyone loves a lover.

HOW OTHERS SEE YOU

Others see you as one who knows how to give and receive love unconditionally. One sees you as a lover. Most see you as compassionate and aware of life's poignancy. Some may see you as a soft touch and try to take advantage of you.

YOUR HOPES AND FEARS

You would like to give and receive love unconditionally, but fear that you may not be able to. The opportunity to love comes to us all. It is not weakness but great strength to risk it. You may fear, or fear for, a lover.

THE OUTCOME

You will encounter or feel the heady excitement of a new love, even in an existing relationship. You may have the chance to experience the joy of giving and receiving with an open heart. Expect a pleasant surprise.

♥ ◆ Two of Hearts

Romance

♥ Two of Hearts:

Romance

YOU

1 You need the clear, nurturing, supportive and heartfelt exchange of emotions that is the gift of a romantic relationship, though a good familial or business relationship may do instead. Learn what romance truly means.

WHAT SURROUNDS YOU

2 You are surrounded by the chance to know the clear, nurturing, supportive and heartfelt emotional exchange that is the mark of a good romantic relationship, though a familial or business relationship may do instead.

WHAT BLOCKS YOU

3 Romance, or the lack of it, blocks progress. Being overly romantic or losing yourself in relationships is as bad as enjoying no romance at all. Do not just be in love with romance. A romantic partner may be the problem.

YOUR FOUNDATION

4

Crucial to your situation is your ability to be part of an open, nurturing and supportive relationship—romantic, familial or business—where heartfelt emotions are exchanged freely. Few things are more valuable.

WHAT IS BEHIND YOU

5

In the past you knew the clear, nurturing, supportive and heartfelt emotional exchange that marks a good romantic, familial or business relationship. That experience has prepared you well for future relationships.

WHAT CROWNS YOU

6

It would be good to know the supportive and heartfelt emotional exchange that marks a good romantic, familial or business relationship. Visualize how your ideal partner will be. Feel how you will feel when you are together.

WHAT IS BEFORE YOU

7

You will soon get the rare chance to know the clear, nurturing, supportive and heartfelt emotional exchange that is the mark of a good romantic, familial or business relationship. Few things are more valuable.

YOUR PERSONA

8

Present yourself as a rare, lucky person who has the ability to be one-half of a good, open, nurturing, supportive relationship—romantic, familial or business—where heartfelt emotions are exchanged freely.

HOW OTHERS SEE YOU

You are loved. Others see your ability to be one-half of an open, nurturing and supportive relationship—romantic, familial or business—where heartfelt emotions are exchanged freely. This is a most valuable quality.

YOUR HOPES AND FEARS

You hope to be in an honest, supportive relationship—romantic, familial or business—where sincere emotions are exchanged freely, but fear you cannot. Do your best to overcome this fear. It is what stops you.

THE OUTCOME

You will get the rare chance to know the clear, nurturing, supportive and heartfelt emotional exchange that is the mark of a good romantic, familial or business relationship. Few things are more valuable.

♥ Three of Hearts

Celebration

♦ Three of Hearts:
Celebration

1

You

You need to feel filled with gratitude for life's gifts and to celebrate with those you care about. Pay attention to the quality of your food and drink. This is a time when enjoying yourself is as important as working hard.

2

What Surrounds You

You are surrounded by supportive friends and the possibility to experience laughter, celebration and hospitality. People and events may remind you to be grateful for the gifts life has given you. You are called to join the dance.

3

What Blocks You

Doing too much or too little celebrating blocks progress. Moderation is needed or there may be nothing to celebrate. Showing too much or too little gratitude may cause trouble. A "party person" may be the problem.

YOUR FOUNDATION

Crucial to your situation is your ability to feel grateful for life's gifts and to celebrate with those you care about. Being able to share with and show gratitude to others is also vital. Find a good place to hold your celebration.

WHAT IS BEHIND YOU

In the past, there was an opportunity to show gratitude for life's gifts and to celebrate with those you cared about. If the opportunity was not taken, time was wasted. Show your gratitude now. Make some time to have fun.

WHAT CROWNS YOU

It would be good to feel grateful for life's gifts and to celebrate with those you care about. Visualize yourself as becoming richer by sharing your life's treasures and expressing gratitude to all. Plan to throw the kind of party you always wanted to go to.

WHAT IS BEFORE YOU

There will soon be the opportunity to celebrate with those you care about and feel filled with gratitude for life's gifts. There may be something great to celebrate. Sharing faith, hope and charity may hearten all concerned.

YOUR PERSONA

Present yourself as feeling filled with gratitude for life's gifts and wanting to celebrate with those you care about. Be a living example of the power of faith, hope and charity. You do not have to appear as serious or responsible

HOW OTHERS SEE YOU

Others see you as feeling filled with gratitude for life's gifts and wanting to celebrate with those you care about. Most see you as trying to balance work and play. A few may see you as more interested in fun than in work.

YOUR HOPES AND FEARS

You hope you can allow yourself to feel filled with gratitude for life's gifts and to celebrate with those you care about, but fear you cannot. You need to let joy wash away your fears. You may fear,or fear for, a "party person."

THE OUTCOME

There will be the opportunity to celebrate with those you care about and to feel filled with gratitude for life's gifts. There may be something wonderful to celebrate. Sharing faith, hope and charity may hearten all concerned.

♥◇ Four of Hearts

Re-evaluation

♥ Four of Hearts:

Re–evaluation

1 YOU

You need to re-evaluate things. If you are bored or dissatisfied with the status quo, avoid distractions and examine your heart of hearts to gain clarity. "Crying over spilt milk" or saying "I told you so" is not attractive.

2 WHAT SURROUNDS YOU

You are surrounded by the need for re-evaluation. You or your work may be re-evaluated. There is either dissatisfaction or boredom with the status quo. Be aware that others may "cry over spilt milk," or say "I told you so."

3 WHAT BLOCKS YOU

Too much or too little re-evaluation blocks you. Constant re-evaluation causes mistrust and instability. Avoiding re-evaluation only postpones pain until the truth is finally revealed. Be careful of saying "I told you so."

YOUR FOUNDATION

4

Crucial to your situation is your ability to re-evaluate things and/or to deal with re-evaluation. Distractions must be avoided, as must fear of what the outcome of this process will produce. Avoid any "crying over spilt milk."

WHAT IS BEHIND YOU

5

In the past, re-evaluation challenged you with painful feelings. If you failed to avoid distraction and to search your "heart of hearts" for answers, you wasted time. Apply the lessons of that time to the present situation.

WHAT CROWNS YOU

6

It would be good to re-evaluate your situation. Visualize your situation but see it as happening to strangers. Are these strangers doing what you know they should be doing? Are they harming others, even unintentionally?

WHAT IS BEFORE YOU

7

You will soon see a need for re-evaluation. You may be re-evaluating the situation. Be aware it may be you who is the subject of the forthcoming re-evaluation. Avoid "crying over spilt milk" or saying "I told you so."

YOUR PERSONA

8

Present yourself as needing to re-evaluate things. If you feel bored or dissatisfied, avoid all distractions and meditate to gain clear insights. You may say "I told you so," but only if it can help avoid future problems.

How Others See You

Others see you as needing to re-evaluate things. You may appear bored or dissatisfied with the status quo. Some may see you as a complainer, someone who says "I told you so," or one who is "crying over spilt milk."

Your Hopes and Fears

You hope you can re-evaluate things and come to know where you stand, but fear you might not be able to. You may fear that you will like the conclusions you come to even less. It must be done. You may be afraid to hear "I told you so."

The Outcome

You will see a need for re-evaluation. You may be re-evaluating the situation. Be aware it may be you who is the subject of the forthcoming re-evaluation. Avoid "crying over spilt milk" or saying "I told you so."

Five of Hearts

Disappointment

◆ Five of Hearts:

Dis-appointment

1

YOU

You need to understand rejection and disappointment. You may feel that you must walk away from someone or something. Realize the ways disappointment gives experience that can help to ensure future success.

2

WHAT SURROUNDS YOU

You are surrounded by feelings of disappointment. You may feel rejection or the desire to walk away from something. Experiencing this kind of emotional pain can give valuable wisdom that can ensure future success.

3

WHAT BLOCKS YOU

Disappointment or rejection blocks progress. You may feel like giving up but should not. Denying disappointment may prevent you from leaving when you should. A disappointed person may be the problem.

YOUR FOUNDATION

4

Crucial to your situation is your ability to feel disappointed, to even walk away from someone or something, but yet realize how loss is an experience that can ensure future success. Dealing with a disappointed person is vital.

WHAT IS BEHIND YOU

5

A disappointment that may have caused the rejection of someone or something is now affecting the present situation. If you can see how this is so, you can put it behind you. If not, do not let the past intrude on the present.

WHAT CROWNS YOU

6

It would be good to accept disappointment. You might have to walk away from someone or something. Visualize yourself walking towards the bright future you desire. Feel as you will when you get there.

WHAT IS BEFORE YOU

7

A time of disappointment or rejection may be drawing near. You may have to walk away from someone, somewhere or something. Be careful and with professional counseling you may avoid it. If not, it can help you avoid depression and despondency.

YOUR PERSONA

8

Present yourself as disappointed and in the process of walking away from someone, somewhere or something. Show you are looking for something new. If you are depressed and despondent, seek professional counseling.

HOW OTHERS SEE YOU

Others see you as disappointed and maybe even heart-broken, depressed or despondent. You seem to be in the process of walking away from someone, somewhere or something. A few think you need professional counseling.

YOUR HOPES AND FEARS

You may hope to avoid the disappointment, rejection, or letting go of someone or something, but fear you may not be able to. If dissapointment comes, learn from it and grow stronger. If fear paralyzes you, seek professional counseling.

THE OUTCOME

The outcome may be a time of disappointment or rejection. You may have to walk away from someone, some-where or something. Be careful and with professional counseling you may avoid it. If not, it can help you avoid depression and despondency.

Joy

♥ ◆ Six of Hearts

♦ Six of Hearts:

Joy

1

You

You need to experience child-like joy. The child you were still lives within you and must be cared for. Allow yourself positive, nostalgic memories of childhood, friends and family. If you can, spend time with younger people.

2

What Surrounds You

You are surrounded by child-like joy. A smell or other stimulus to your senses may send you into a nostalgic reverie where memories of childhood friends and family dwell. A child-like, joyful person may help or need help.

3

What Blocks You

Too much playfulness, or a lack of it, blocks progress. Inappropriate or childish behavior can work against you. You may be ignoring the child that dwells within who needs love and fun. Children or your past may pose problems.

YOUR FOUNDATION

Crucial to your situation is your ability to value and experience child-like joy, nostalgia and the non-judgmental, undemanding friendship of youth. Dealing with the joyfulness of a child is vital. Spend time with younger people.

WHAT IS BEHIND YOU

In the past, you knew true child-like joy. The nostalgia you feel for your youth, old friends or "the old days" re-establishes your connection to your inner child. Behavior patterns born of your childhood may be waning.

WHAT CROWNS YOU

It would be good to feel child-like joy and nostalgia for childhood, old friends and family. Visualize yourself experiencing your fondest childhood memories. Savor each one, experiencing them with all your senses.

WHAT IS BEFORE YOU

You will soon experience child-like joy. Your senses may trigger a nostalgic reverie where memories of childhood, friends and family delight you. A child or someone from your past may reappear in your life now. Play more.

YOUR PERSONA

Present yourself as someone who values the innocence, wisdom and the truthfulness of youth. Show you understand child-like joy, feelings of nostalgia, family life, loyalty and friendship. Be aware of your "inner child."

How Others See You

Others see you as someone who values the innocence, wisdom and truthfulness of youth. They see you understand child-like joy, feelings of nostalgia, family life, loyalty and friendship, and love your own inner child.

Your Hopes and Fears

You hope you can feel joy with the purity of your nostalgic memories of childhood, friends and family, but fear you may not be able to. You may fear painful memories of paradise lost. Or, you may fear having responsibility for a child.

The Outcome

You will experience child-like joy. Your senses may trigger a nostalgic reverie in which memories of childhood, friends and family delight you. A child or someone from your past may reappear in your life now. Play more.

Illusion

♦♥ Seven of Hearts

♦ **Seven of Hearts:**

Illusion

1

YOU

You need to separate what is real from what is an illusion. Protect against unclear or wishful thinking. Learn the power of your sleeping and waking dreams. Avoid intoxication and escapism. Do not decide until you are sure.

2

WHAT SURROUNDS YOU

You are surrounded by too many choices and the confusion between what is real and what is an illusion. Do not act until you are more certain. You may be surrounded by intoxication and escapism. An intoxicated person may help or, more likely, need help.

3

WHAT BLOCKS YOU

Illusion blocks your progress. Illusion and fantasy can be useful as sources of invention and creativity, but avoid deception and escapism. Too many choices or wishful thinking can also obscure your path. Avoid intoxication in all forms. An intoxicated person may be the problem.

YOUR FOUNDATION

Crucial to your situation is your ability to separate what is real from what is an illusion. Wait until you are more certain before deciding how to proceed. Avoid intoxication, escapism and confusion, and people suffering from those things.

WHAT IS BEHIND YOU

In the past, you saw the results of either intoxication or too many choices. If reality was not separated from illusion and inspiration from pipedreams, time was wasted. Be practical and you can make your inspirations real.

WHAT CROWNS YOU

It would be good to be able to separate what is real from what is an illusion. Visualize yourself being inspired by the attractive choices around you but delaying action until your head and your heart agree which is best for you.

WHAT IS BEFORE YOU

You will soon encounter illusion, confusion or distraction. Avoid intoxication and other forms of escapism. Distinguish creative inspiration from pipedreams. Postpone decisions until you are sure what is best to do. It is a good time for fantasizing, not decision-making.

YOUR PERSONA

Present yourself as trying to separate reality from illusion. Be clear that you cannot decide until you are sure. Act inspired by your many choices but uncommitted to any one of them. You may have to wear a disguise.

How Others See You

Others see you as confused and possibly intoxicated. Some see you as inspired by a great creative spirit. Others see you as just a daydreamer who is totally unrealistic. A few think you are hiding something.

Your Hopes and Fears

You hope you can distinguish reality from illusion, but fear you may not be able to. You may fear to dream or delve into your psychological makeup. Avoid intoxication and escapism completely. You may fear having to hide.

The Outcome

You will soon encounter illusion, confusion or distraction. Avoid intoxication and other forms of escapism. Distinguish creative inspiration from pipedreams. Postpone decisions until you are sure what is best to do. It is a good time for fantasizing, not decision-making.

Sacrifice

♦ **Eight of Hearts**

Sacrifice

YOU

You need to be more aware of the physical, mental or emotional sacrifices that are or will become involved in the present situation. You may need to seek a cause more worthy of your efforts and sacrifice. You need to heal.

WHAT SURROUNDS YOU

You are surrounded by the chance to become more aware of the physical, emotional, or mental sacrifices that are or will become involved in the present situation. The gain must be worth the loss involved.

WHAT BLOCKS YOU

Sacrifice, or a lack of it, blocks your progress. The cause may not be worthy. Physical, mental or emotional resources may be drained. Needed sacrifice may not be made by you or others. Sacrifices may be ignored, causing resentment.

YOUR FOUNDATION

4 Crucial to your situation is your awareness of the physical, mental or emotional sacrifices that are or will become involved in the present circumstances. Determine if the cause is worthy of the sacrifices required.

WHAT IS BEHIND YOU

5 Past sacrifices affect the present situation. Focusing on the concerns of others may have left you unfulfilled and drained physically, mentally, emotionally or financially. You need not sacrifice again in the near future.

WHAT CROWNS YOU

6 It would be good to be more aware of the physical, mental or emotional sacrifices that are or will become involved in your situation. Visualize the possible gains and sacrifices required on the pans of a balance scale.

WHAT IS BEFORE YOU

7 You may soon be required to be more aware of the physical, mental or emotional sacrifices that are or will become involved in the present situation. A more worthy cause or direction may have to be found. You need to heal.

YOUR PERSONA

8 Present yourself as one who is aware of the physical, mental or emotional sacrifices that are or will become involved in the present situation. Show that you can determine if the cause is worthy of these sacrifices.

How Others See You

Others see you as aware of and affected by the physical, mental or emotional sacrifices that are or will become involved in the present situation. You may seem hurt, exploited, drained or unfulfilled.

Your Hopes and Fears

You hope you can avoid making sacrifices that produce results that are unworthy of your loss, but you fear you may not be able to. The outcome of your situation will determine if it was worth what has been sacrificed.

The Outcome

You may be required to be more aware of the physical, mental or emotional sacrifices that are or will become involved in the present situation. A more worthy cause or direction may have to be found. You need to heal.

Nine of Hearts

Fulfillment

♦ Nine of hearts:

Fulfillment

YOU

1

Your need to know what fulfillment really is. A wish may be granted, but in its own time and, perhaps, in an unexpected way. Be sure to wish for what is best for you and yours, for you will probably get what you want.

WHAT SURROUNDS YOU

2

You are surrounded by the chance to have your wish granted in a happy way. It may come in an unexpected way or after a small delay, but know that this is a very lucky time for you. The chance to know fulfillment is real.

WHAT BLOCKS YOU

3

Fulfillment, or a lack of it, blocks progress. Present goals may not be in your best interest. A wish fulfilled or fulfilled too easily may not satisfy. Expecting things to happen a certain way keeps you from seeing alternatives.

YOUR FOUNDATION

4 Crucial to your situation is your awareness of the many ways the present situation is the fulfillment of past dreams and wishes. Focus on what you have, not on what you lack. You may receive a gift or see a wish fulfilled.

WHAT IS BEHIND YOU

5 In the past, you got your wish. It may have happened in an unexpected way. You may not be aware that your wish has been fulfilled, but it can empower you if you take the time now to see how this is so.

WHAT CROWNS YOU

6 It would be good to be aware of the many ways you have had your past wishes fulfilled. Visualize yourself with a Genie who has granted these wishes and will now grant another. Wish for what you really, really want.

WHAT IS BEFORE YOU

7 You will soon see your wish granted in a happy way. Be alert to it happening in an unexpected way. Be sure to wish for what you really want because you will probably get it. You are "lucky" now and can get what you want if you ask for it in the right way.

YOUR PERSONA

8 Present yourself as a fortunate person who feels content, satisfied and fulfilled. Show you are aware that you have had your wishes granted. Make it clear you want to help others get their wishes granted, too.

How Others See You

Others see you as a fortunate person who feels content, satisfied and fulfilled. They see you are aware of the many ways your wishes have been granted. They see you as lucky. They may see you as a good luck charm.

Your Hopes and Fears

You hope your wishes will be fulfilled, but fear they will not be granted or that the result of their being granted will bring trouble. Wish for what is best for all concerned. You may fear that prayers will not be heard.

The Outcome

You will see your wish granted in a happy way. Be alert to it happening in an unexpected way. Be sure to wish for what you really want because you will probably get it. You are "lucky" now and can get what you want if you ask for it in the right way.

Success

♥ Ten of Hearts:

Success

1 YOU

You need to be more aware of how successful and respected you are. You will never gain more than you have now until you empower yourself by appreciating what you have done. Success is really how you define it.

2 WHAT SURROUNDS YOU

You have an air of success around you. You are in a place where you can attain a goal that can bring lasting personal success and domestic happiness. You are respected. A successful person may help or need help.

3 WHAT BLOCKS YOU

Success, or a lack of it, blocks progress. Too much success can make it difficult to cope with failure. Lack of success or reputation can be depressing and weaken efforts. Envy or a successful person may be the problem.

Your Foundation

Crucial to your situation is your awareness of how successful and respected you are. To attain greater success,
empower yourself by appreciating what you have done
and showing it. Dealing with the success of others is vital.

What is Behind You

In the past, you were successful and respected for it. Your
reputation is solid. Successful dealings with friends, relatives
and business associates can help you now. The influence of
a successful person may be waning.

What Crowns You

It would be good to be more aware of how successful and
respected you are. Visualize the goals you have attained
and those who would be thrilled just to have what you
have. Feel the love of those wishing you success.

What is Before You

You will soon be aware of how successful and respected
you are. You may attain a goal that brings lasting happiness. Your reputation may be enhanced. You may win an
award. A successful person may be involved.

Your Persona

Present yourself as someone who is aware of the many
ways you are successful and respected. Act as if you have
attained a major life goal and found your spiritual family.
Be kind and gracious to avoid the envy of others.

How Others See You

Others see you as someone who is successful and respected. They see you have found your spiritual family. Most see your life's story as one to be emulated. The jealous few may see you as flaunting your success in their faces.

Your Hopes and Fears

You may hope to be considered successful by yourself and others, but fear you may not. You may fear that if you do attain success, the price of attaining it will be too high. You may fear, or fear for, a successful person.

The Outcome

You will become aware of how successful and respected you are. You may attain a goal that brings lasting happiness, or you may win an award. Your reputation may be enhanced. A successful person may be involved.

◆ ♥ Princess of Hearts

Tenderness

♥ Princess of Hearts:

Tenderness

1

YOU

You need to concentrate on the communication of tender feelings, hunches and dreams. You are "pregnant" with romantic ideas and idealized fancies. Balance logic and intuition and you will see them born in your life.

2

WHAT SURROUNDS YOU

You are surrounded by the need to place more importance on the communication of feelings, intuitions and dreams. It can be a romantic time if you let it be so. A tender, sensitive person may help or need help.

3

WHAT BLOCKS YOU

Being too tender, or not tender enough, blocks progress. Too much tenderness may make a person too soft. Tenderness withheld or misplaced can cause insecurity and delay growth. A sensitive person may be the problem.

YOUR FOUNDATION

Crucial to your situation is your ability to value and communicate feelings, intuitions and dreams. Your ability to handle news of an emotional nature is vital. Dealing with the tenderness and sensitivity of a young person is also important.

WHAT IS BEHIND YOU

In the past, the communication of feelings, intuitions and dreams were major issues. Lessons learned then can affect the present for good or ill. The influence of a tender or sensitive person may be waning.

WHAT CROWNS YOU

It would be good to communicate feelings, intuitions and dreams. Visualize yourself pregnant with these tender feelings. Now see yourself giving birth to them, ushering them into a loving world that needs and wants them.

WHAT IS BEFORE YOU

You will soon encounter or have to act as someone who is skilled in the communication of love, feelings, dreams or intuitions. You may have to deal with the tenderness of a young person. You may "give birth" to something.

YOUR PERSONA

Present yourself as a tender person. Show your concern with the communication of feelings, intuitions and dreams. Dress fancifully. Be the rare romantic who does not reflexively let emotions overrule logic.

HOW OTHERS SEE YOU

Others see you as a tender, helpful person. Most see you as concerned with the communication of feelings, intuitions and dreams. Some may think you too romantic, lazy and dependent on others. A few question your sense of style.

YOUR HOPES AND FEARS

You hope feelings, intuitions and dreams will bear valuable fruit, but fear there might not be the emotional maturity necessary. You may fear pregnancy or giving birth. You may fear, or fear for, a sensitive person.

THE OUTCOME

You will encounter or have to act as someone who is skilled in the communication of love, feelings, dreams or intuitions. You may have to deal with the tenderness of a young person. You may "give birth" to something.

Prince of Hearts

Charm

◆ Prince of Hearts :

Charm

YOU

1

You need to be charming and attractive to others, regardless of their sex, while still expressing the romantic, poetic view of life in your own unique way. You may be in love with love itself. You need to explore your sexuality carefully.

WHAT SURROUNDS YOU

2

You are surrounded by emotions and emotional people. The charm of a romantic, poetic view of life is attracting you. Avoid liars or over-embellishments of the truth. Sexuality must be explored carefully. A charming person may help or need help.

WHAT BLOCKS YOU

3

Charm, or a lack of it, can block your progress. Too much charm can appear insincere, even if heartfelt. Lack of charm and romance makes life dull. Sexuality may cause trouble. A charming young person may be the problem.

Your Foundation

Crucial to your situation is your ability to be charming and attractive to others, regardless of their sex, while still expressing the romantic and poetic view of life in your own unique way. Dealing with the charm of a young person is vital.

What is Behind You

In the past, being charming and attractive to others, regardless of their sex, and expressing the romantic, poetic view of life caused you to learn lessons that can be applied now. A charming person's influence may be waning.

What Crowns You

It would be good to be charming and attractive to others, expressing a loving, romantic and poetic view of life's mystery. Visualize yourself in a scene from your favorite romance. Feel every feeling you can. Savor them.

What is Before You

You will soon encounter or have to act as someone who is very charming and attractive to others, regardless of their sex. A romantic spirit with a poetic view of love and life can take you far. Sexuality will be explored carefully.

Your Persona

Present yourself as being charming and attractive to others, regardless of their sex, while still expressing a loving, romantic and poetic view of life. Explore your sexuality carefully. Do so in a way that your secrets are not revealed.

HOW OTHERS SEE YOU

9

Others see you as being charming and attractive to every-one, regardless of their sex, and expressing a romantic view of life. To some you may seem to be promising too much. A few see you exploring your sexuality carefully.

YOUR HOPES AND FEARS

10

You hope you can be charming and attractive to others, regardless of their sex, while still expressing a romantic and poetic view of life, but fear your actions will be misunderstood. You may fear exploring your sexuality.

THE OUTCOME

11

You will encounter or have to act as someone who is very charming and attractive to others, regardless of their sex. A romantic spirit with a poetic view of love and life can take you far. Sexuality will be explored carefully.

Empathy

♥ Queen of Hearts

♦ Queen of Hearts: *Empathy*

 1

YOU

You need to empathize with human frailty, yours included. Think with your heart, not your head. Learn how those in need cope with life's challenges and share your knowledge. Be aware of getting too close. Hug someone you care about.

 2

WHAT SURROUNDS YOU

You are surrounded by an air of empathy for human frailty. Secrets may be kept in an effort to be helpful. An empathetic person may help or need help, though they may give the appearance of wanting to meddle.

 3

WHAT BLOCKS YOU

Empathy, or a lack of it, can block your progress. Too much empathy makes clear thinking impossible. Its lack prevents the true picture from being known and wastes time. An overly-sensitive person may be the problem.

YOUR FOUNDATION

Crucial to your situation is your ability to be empathetic to human frailty. You may have to learn and/or teach how those in need cope with life's ups and downs. Give a hand, not a handout. An empathetic person may be important now.

WHAT IS BEHIND YOU

In the past, you learned about suffering and the costs and benefits of being empathetic to human frailty. Apply what you learned then to your present situation. The influence of an empathetic person may be waning.

WHAT CROWNS YOU

It would be good to be empathetic to human frailty. Visualize yourself as the person you are trying to understand. See yourself actually living their life from their point of view. Experience what it feels like and remember it later.

WHAT IS BEFORE YOU

You may soon encounter or have to act as someone who is empathetic to human frailty. You may soon have to learn and/or teach how those in need cope with life's ups and downs. An empathetic person may become important.

YOUR PERSONA

Present yourself as empathetic to human frailty. Show you know how those in need cope with life's ups and downs. You may want to teach others how to cope. If so, be sure to give them a hand, not a handout.

HOW OTHERS SEE YOU

Others see you as empathetic to human frailty. They see you know how those in need cope with life's ups and downs. You seem willing to share your knowledge. A few may see you as too secretive or too meddlesome.

YOUR HOPES AND FEARS

You hope to solve others' problems, but fear what will happen, whether you do or do not. You may fear smothering the initiative of those you help and appearing meddlesome. You may fear getting close. You may fear or fear for an empathetic person.

THE OUTCOME

You may encounter or have to act as someone who is empathetic to human frailty. You may soon have to learn and/or teach how those in need cope with life's ups and downs. An empathetic person may become important.

Consideration

♦ ♥ King of Hearts

♥ king of Hearts:

Consideration

1 | YOU

You need to be considerate as you counsel others. You may need to understand why strong feelings have surfaced and how to best cope with them. Do not repress emotions. You must see your life as a work of art.

2 | WHAT SURROUNDS YOU

You are surrounded by consideration and the ability to counsel others wisely. Though someone may be jealous, emotions can now be understood and dealt with. An advisor, a healer or an artist may help or need help.

3 | WHAT BLOCKS YOU

Consideration, or a lack of it, can block progress. Too much consideration is seen as weakness by those who do not deserve it. Inconsideration or jealousy can hurt you. An advisor, a healer or an artist may cause a problem.

YOUR FOUNDATION

Crucial to your situation is your ability to be considerate and counsel others while feeling and dealing with strong emotions. An understanding of the arts and humanities is needed. An advisor, a healer or an artist may be important.

WHAT IS BEHIND YOU

In the past, the ability to be considerate and counsel others while feeling and dealing with strong emotions was tested. The results of that test must be applied now. The influence of an advisor, healer or artist may be waning.

WHAT CROWNS YOU

It would be good to be considerate and counsel others wisely while feeling and dealing with strong emotions. Visualize yourself as a protective shepherd to your flock of loved ones. Do not resent others who also offer their help.

WHAT IS BEFORE YOU

You will soon encounter or have to act like someone who knows how to be an advisor, a healer or an artist. Be the ruler of your emotions, seeking to understand, not repress them. Study the life and teachings of a master or philosopher.

YOUR PERSONA

Present yourself as the ruler of your emotions. Show you are a wise and considerate counselor seeking to understand strong emotions. Appreciate the arts and philosophy. Demonstrate your unique style of creative ability.

How Others See You

Others see you as the ruler of your emotions, a considerate counselor seeking to handle strong feelings creatively. If you are jealous, you deal with your inner turmoil. Some see you as an advisor, a healer or an artist.

Your Hopes and Fears

You hope you can be a considerate counselor, able to deal with strong emotions creatively, but fear you may not. You may fear the effects of jealousy. You may fear, or fear for, an advisor, a healer or an artist.

The Outcome

You will encounter or have to act like someone who knows how to be an advisor, a healer or an artist. Be the ruler of your emotions, seeking to understand, not repress them. Study the life and teachings of a master or philosopher.

Ace of Pentacles

Reward

✦ Ace of Pentacles:

Reward

1 You

You need to attain a new level of material wealth and earthly power. It may come to you as the materialization of an idea, a gift, inheritance, bonus, promotion or other reward. The chance for financial gain is real.

2 What Surrounds You

You are surrounded by the materialization of wealth and earthly power. If you learn and apply the lessons of this reading, you may be able to claim your rich reward. The chance for new financial gain is real.

3 What Blocks You

Reward, or a lack of it, blocks progress. Focusing on the reward that could be gained may distract from the job at hand. Lack of reward makes it harder for one to keep trying. A reward might not be as expected.

YOUR FOUNDATION

Crucial to your situation is your ability to believe you now have enough resources to accomplish your goal. This is an ancient technique and it works. A new beginning regarding tangible wealth, power and practical affairs is here.

WHAT IS BEHIND YOU

In the past, a long-held desire became real. It was a reward for wisdom and dedication. Much positive energy was created. Draw on that energy and on what was learned from that time of reward. Call in favors.

WHAT CROWNS YOU

It would be good to see a long-held desire become real as a reward for wisdom and dedication. Visualize the law of cause and effect working to give you what you deserve. Know that visualization produces rich rewards.

WHAT IS BEFORE YOU

You will soon enjoy a rich reward, though it may come in a form that is hard for you to see. If you have prepared correctly, much profit and wealth may accrue. You must realize that you have earned it, whether or not anyone thinks you have.

YOUR PERSONA

Present yourself as a very prosperous person who has enjoyed many rewards and can show others how to obtain their own. Show you have a new opportunity for financial gain. Act as if you have the golden touch.

How Others See You

Others see you as a very successful person who has enjoyed many rewards and can show others how to obtain their own. They see you represent a new opportunity for big financial gains. It is as if you have the golden touch.

Your Hopes and Fears

You hope you will enjoy a rich reward, but are afraid you may not receive or deserve it. You may fear you could not handle the changes that would happen if you got what you desire. You may fear success or being wealthy.

The Outcome

You will enjoy a rich reward, though it may come in a form that is hard for you to see. If you have prepared well, much profit and wealth may accrue. You must realize that you have earned it, whether or not anyone thinks you have.

◆★ Two of Pentacles

Change

◆ Two of Pentacles:

Change

1 ## YOU

You need to be able to cope with change. For now, it might be better to keep two or more things going at once rather than focus on one. You must stay centered while you stay flexible and keep informed. Know thyself.

2 ## WHAT SURROUNDS YOU

You are surrounded by rapid and constant change and instability. You cannot depend on anything to stay the same for very long. You must stay centered or be tossed about. A changeable person may help or need help.

3 ## WHAT BLOCKS YOU

Change, or a lack of it, blocks progress. Too much change makes it impossible to plan or feel secure. Lack of change is boring and causes change to come about in unpleasant ways. A changeable person may be the problem.

YOUR FOUNDATION

4 Crucial to your situation is your ability to cope with change or a changeable person. It is an unstable time. You must function without a secure home base. You must stay centered as you stay flexible, versatile and informed.

WHAT IS BEHIND YOU

5 In the past, changeable conditions required you stay flexible and informed. It was vital to keep two or more things going at once rather than focus on one. Apply that lesson. A changeable person's influence maybe waning.

WHAT CROWNS YOU

6 It would be good to be versatile and handle change well. Visualize yourself as the eye of a hurricane, always calm and quiet no matter how fast the howling winds swirl around you.

WHAT IS BEFORE YOU

7 You will soon encounter a period of change and instability. You may have to focus on two or more things at once. Stay centered and informed even as you keep flexible and versatile. A fickle person may be involved.

YOUR PERSONA

8 Present yourself as versatile, flexible and able to change as the situation requires. Show it is not the time for you to commit to anything, so you have decided to be involved with whatever or whomever you are interested in.

How Others See You

Others see you as versatile, flexible and able to change as the situation requires. They see you are trying to juggle two or more things at the same time. Some may see you as fickle, two-faced or lacking commitment.

Your Hopes and Fears

You hope you can cope with change and instability, but fear you may not. You may fear losing control. You may be afraid this situation will never resolve itself completely. You may fear, or fear for, a changeable person.

The Outcome

You will soon encounter a period of change and instability. You may have to focus on two or more things at once. Stay centered and informed, even as you keep flexible and versatile. A changeable person may be involved.

Work

★ Three of Pentacles

Work

YOU

1 You need to do work that is satisfying to you. Think of your work as tending your garden. You may need help. It may be beneficial to share your work with a partner, but only if they are as conscientious as you.

WHAT SURROUNDS YOU

2 You are surrounded by the chance to do work that can be satisfying. Think of your work as tending your garden. There are like-minded people around you. A co-worker or a service provider may help or need help.

WHAT BLOCKS YOU

3 Work, or a lack of it, blocks progress. Too much work or work you dislike can make life seem miserable. Lack of work destroys self-esteem. A co-worker or service provider may be the problem.

YOUR FOUNDATION

4

Crucial to your situation is your ability to do work that is satisfying. Work must be thought of as tending a garden. Work with like-minded people. Dealing with the work ethic of a co-worker or a service provider is vital.

WHAT IS BEHIND YOU

5

In the past, you were able to do work that was satisfying. It was as if your work was like tending your garden. That attitude and the ability to work with others can help you now. A co-worker's influence may be waning.

WHAT CROWNS YOU

6

It would be good to be doing work that is satisfying. Visualize your work as caring for your garden. See yourself preparing the soil, planting, weeding and reaping the harvest. Know help is available. If you want it, ask for it.

WHAT IS BEFORE YOU

7

You will soon have the opportunity to do work that is satisfying. It will be like tending a garden. It may benefit you to work with others if they are as conscientious as you. A co-worker or service provider may be involved.

YOUR PERSONA

8

Present yourself as someone who enjoys your chosen line of work. Show you are willing to roll up your sleeves and do it yourself, but are a team player when others work as hard. Demonstrate your ability to give service.

How Others See You

Others see you as enjoying your chosen line of work. They see you are willing to roll up your sleeves and do it yourself, but are a team player when others work as hard. Some may see you as a servant.

Your Hopes and Fears

You hope you can do work that is satisfying to you, but fear you may not be able to. You may fear to try and make this dream come true. You may fear being a servant. You may fear, or fear for, a co-worker or a service provider.

The Outcome

You will have the opportunity to do work that is satisfying. It will be like tending a garden. It may benefit you to work with others if they are as conscientious as you. A co-worker or service provider may be involved.

★ Four of Pentacles

Possessiveness

★ Four of Pentacles:

Possessivenes

1

YOU

You need to hold on to what you have. Manage and guard it carefully. Things must be put in order and in proper perspective. Reflect on your self-worth and what is valuable to you. It is time to think like an executive.

2

WHAT SURROUNDS YOU

You are surrounded by those who believe in holding onto what they have. Though their management skills are high, as is their concern with security, they put their needs first. An executive type may help or need help.

3

WHAT BLOCKS YOU

Possessiveness, or a lack of it, blocks progress. We are caretakers, not owners of the things we have and those we love. Holding on too tight or letting go too easily are equally wrong. An executive may be the problem.

YOUR FOUNDATION

Crucial to your situation is your ability to hold on to what you have. Manage and guard it carefully. Put things in order and in perspective. Guard against selfishness and greed. Dealing with the ways of an executive is vital.

WHAT IS BEHIND YOU

In the past, you held onto what you had. You may have managed and protected it well, but selfishness on your part can now come back to haunt you. Put things in perspective. An executive's influence may be waning.

WHAT CROWNS YOU

It would be good to manage and protect what you are responsible for. Visualize yourself as the righteous care-taker of your charges. Feel protective forces helping you to do it well. Know the joy of responsibility.

WHAT IS BEFORE YOU

You will soon have to evaluate the wisdom of holding on to what you have. Good management is emphasized. Retain and protect that which reflects your true values and what you need in order to grow. An executive type may be involved.

YOUR PERSONA

Present yourself as conservative in the best sense of the word. Show that your priorities are in order and that you can manage and protect what you are responsible for. Show high self-worth. Act like an executive.

How Others See You

Others see you as conservative, determined to hold on to what you have. Most see you as protective of what you are responsible for and a good manager. You seem like executive material. A few see you as greedy.

Your Hopes and Fears

You hope you will be able to hold on to what you have, managing and protecting what you are responsible for, but fear that doing so may divert you from exciting new opportunities. You may fear to appear greedy. You may fear, or fear for, an executive.

The Outcome

You will have to evaluate the wisdom of holding on to what you have. Good management is emphasized. That which is necessary for growth or a reflection of your true values should be retained and protected. An executive type may be involved.

Five of Pentacles

Anxiety

◆★ Five of Pentacles:

Anxiety

1

YOU

You need to learn to cope with stress and anxiety. Worries can paralyze your actions until you face their source, focus on the present and do what you can with what you have now. Stress management is a vital concern.

2

WHAT SURROUNDS YOU

You are surrounded by an atmosphere of stress and anxiety. Worries can paralyze action. Their source must be faced before all can get busy doing what they can with what they have. An anxious person may help or need help.

3

WHAT BLOCKS YOU

Anxiety, or denial of it, blocks progress. Worry causes stress which impacts health and reduces efficiency. Repressing anxiety when there is reason for concern delays corrective actions. An anxious person may be the problem.

YOUR FOUNDATION

4

Crucial to your situation is your ability to cope with stress and anxiety. Worries can paralyze your actions until you face their source and get busy doing what you can with what you have. Dealing with an anxious person is vital.

WHAT IS BEHIND YOU

5

In the past, you experienced stress and anxiety. Unless you faced their source, focused on the present and did what you could with what you had, your effectiveness has been hurt. An anxious person's influence may be waning.

WHAT CROWNS YOU

6

It would be good to cope with stress and anxiety. Visualize yourself facing your worries. Ask them what they are trying to protect you from. Listen closely to what they tell you. Thank them and get on with your life.

WHAT IS BEFORE YOU

7

You will soon have to cope with stress, anxiety or denial. Worries paralyze your actions until you face their source, focus on the present moment and do what you can with what you have. An anxious person may be involved.

YOUR PERSONA

8

Present yourself as having to cope with stress and anxiety. Let others know you are at a difficult time in your life. It is not weakness, but the greatest strength to ask for their help. If they avoid you, move on and find out who your friends are.

How Others See You

Others see that you have to cope with stress and anxiety. You have them worried. They can tell you are hurting. They may be worried that they cannot do enough to help. Some may avoid you because of it.

Your Hopes and Fears

You hope you can cope with stress and anxiety, but fear you may not be able to. You may be afraid of being afraid. Focus on what you are doing now, not on the past or future. You may fear, or fear for, an anxious person.

The Outcome

You will have to cope with stress, anxiety or denial. Worries can paralyze your actions until you face their source, focus on the present and do what you can with what you have. An anxious person may be involved.

Generosity

Six of Pentacles

◆ Six of Pentacles:

Generosity

1

YOU

You need to experience real generosity. Fulfillment is found through sharing. Drop all pretenses. Give of yourself and from your heart, if you can. If not, ask for what you need. Be thankful for the generosity of others.

2

WHAT SURROUNDS YOU

You are surrounded by the spirit of generosity, sharing and riches. There must be no pretenses. You have only to ask and it will be given to you. Give what you can to others. A generous person may help or need help.

3

WHAT BLOCKS YOU

Generosity, or a lack of it, blocks progress. Receiving too much kills initiative. Giving too much or to those not worthy drains resources. Withholding needed help creates bad karma. A generous person may be the problem.

YOUR FOUNDATION

Crucial to your situation is real generosity. Fulfillment is found through sharing. Drop all pretenses. Give of yourself from your heart, if you can. If not, ask for what you need. Dealing with the generosity of others is vital.

WHAT IS BEHIND YOU

In the past, you saw what real generosity is. Fulfillment was found through sharing. All pretense was dropped as all gave what they could. Renew that spirit of generosity. The influence of a generous person may be waning.

WHAT CROWNS YOU

It would be good to manifest real generosity. Visualize yourself giving what you can to those who deserve it. Now see your gifts return to you twofold, not from those you have given to, but from divine sources.

WHAT IS BEFORE YOU

You will soon manifest real generosity. Sharing will bring fulfillment. All pretenses will be dropped. You will receive what you ask for. If you can, repay this gift by passing it on. A generous person may become involved.

YOUR PERSONA

Present yourself as a generous person, willing to give what you can from your heart to the deserving. Drop all pretenses. If you are in need, ask and it will be given to you. Give aid to a charitable cause.

How Others See You

Others see you as a generous person who is willing to give what you can from your heart to the deserving. They know you are not pretentious. They want to be generous to you. The unscrupulous see you as a cornucopia.

Your Hopes and Fears

You hope you will manifest real generosity in your life, but fear you may not. You may fear you do not have enough to share. Your pride might be deterring you from help. You may fear, or fear for, a generous person.

The Outcome

You will manifest real generosity. Sharing will bring fulfillment. All pretenses will be dropped. You will receive what you ask for. If you can, repay this gift by passing it on. A generous person may become involved.

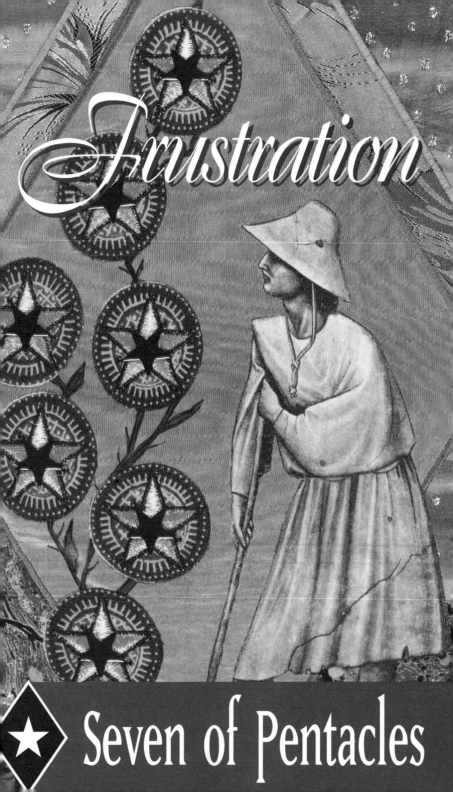

Frustration

★◆ Seven of Pentacles

◆ Seven of Pentacles

Frustration

YOU

You need to cope with frustration. If hard work has not paid off as you planned, remember that expectations are almost always unreasonable. There are no guarantees. Be grateful, focus on the present and do what you can with what you have.

WHAT SURROUNDS YOU

You are surrounded by feelings of frustration, impotence and ingratitude. Expect nothing. Count your blessings, focus on the present and do what you can with what you have. A frustrating person may help or need help.

WHAT BLOCKS YOU

Frustration blocks you. Expectations are almost always unreasonable. Frustration results from feeling ungrateful or impotent. Denied frustration can delay needed change. A frustrating person may be the problem.

YOUR FOUNDATION

4 Crucial to your situation is your ability to cope with feelings of frustration, impotence and ingratitude. Count your blessings, focus on the present and do what you can with what you have now. Dealing with a frustrating person is vital.

WHAT IS BEHIND YOU

5 In the past, you faced feelings of frustration, impotence and ingratitude. If you learned gratitude for what you had and kept trying, frustration will now be behind you. The influence of a frustrated person may be waning.

WHAT CROWNS YOU

6 It would be good to cope with feelings of frustration, impotence and ingratitude. Visualize all of your blessings. Now see the many times you thought you could never attain them. Know you are more powerful now.

WHAT IS BEFORE YOU

7 You will soon have to cope with feelings of frustration, impotence and ingratitude. Count your blessings. Focus on the present moment. Do what you can with what you have. More hard work is needed before you see results. A frustrating person may become involved.

YOUR PERSONA

8 Present yourself as feeling frustrated and impotent in the face of present circumstances. If you can remember to be grateful for what is good, you will triumph. Try not to appear ungrateful. Use criticism constructively.

HOW OTHERS SEE YOU

Others see you as feeling frustrated and impotent in the face of present circumstances. You seem afraid of failure and too worried about the future. You may also seem ungrateful and overly critical.

YOUR HOPES AND FEARS

You hope to cope with feelings of frustration, impotence and ingratitude, but fear you cannot. Focus on the present. Do what you can with what you have and be grateful. You may fear, or fear for, a frustrating person.

THE OUTCOME

You will have to cope with feelings of frustration, impotence and ingratitude. Count your blessings. Focus on the present moment. Do what you can with what you have. More hard work is needed before you see results. A frustrating person may become involved.

Craftsmanship

◆★ **Eight of Pentacles:**

Crafts-manship

1 YOU

You need to approach your situation like a skilled craftsperson would. Study your subject, learn as you work, attend to all details with love and skill, and avoid perfectionism. Do not think about results or rewards.

2 WHAT SURROUNDS YOU

You are surrounded by an air of talent and recognition for it. The methods for realizing your goals are available, if you would only learn them from the experts around you now. A skilled craftsperson may help or need help.

3 WHAT BLOCKS YOU

Craftsmanship, or a lack of it, blocks progress. You may be too much of a perfectionist and not enough of a practical person. Lack of detail and artistry may make things look crude. A finicky person may be the problem.

YOUR FOUNDATION

Crucial to your situation is the level of learning, skill and artistry you possess. If there is a high level of all three, there will be success, as long as perfectionism is avoided. Dealing with the skill of a craftsperson is vital.

WHAT IS BEHIND YOU

In the past, you saw the gain resulting from the best use of talent and attending to details. If there was too much perfectionism, time was wasted. Use perfection as a goal. A craftsperson's influence may be waning.

WHAT CROWNS YOU

It would be good to deal with your situation as a skilled craftsperson would. Visualize each element of your situation as a brick which you examine closely as you build your home. Be a skilled mason and live well.

WHAT IS BEFORE YOU

You will soon encounter or manifest the skill, dedication, attention to details and great results of a talented craftsperson. To succeed, avoid perfectionism and think only of the task at hand. A finicky person may become involved.

YOUR PERSONA

Present yourself as a skilled and dedicated person who has proved that you are a master at your chosen line of work. Show you are attentive to details without being a perfectionist.. Appreciate the finer things in life.

How Others See You

Others see you as a skilled and dedicated person who has demonstrated mastery of your chosen line of work. They see you are attentive to details. A few may see you as a finicky perfectionist more interested in what is wrong than what is right.

Your Hopes and Fears

You hope you can demonstrate mastery at your chosen line of work, but fear you may not really be good enough. To succeed, avoid perfectionism and think only of the task at hand. You may fear, or fear for, a craftsperson or a perfectionist.

The Outcome

You will encounter or manifest the skill, dedication, attention to details and quality results of a talented craftsperson. To succeed, avoid perfectionism and think only of the task at hand. A finicky person may become involved.

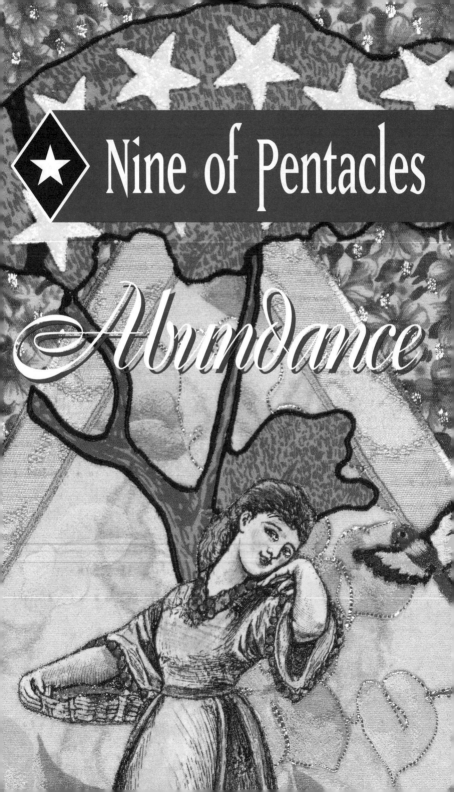

◆⭐ Nine of Pentacles

Abundance

◆ Nine of Pentacles:

Abundance

1 YOU

You need to be self-reliant, independent and free. Learn about your body and how Mother Nature provides all that is needed. Treat your health as your greatest wealth. Get out into the natural world and do your part.

2 WHAT SURROUNDS YOU

You are surrounded by an air of independence, self-reliance and abundance. Your wealth can be increased in many ways. An increase in health is an increase in wealth. Your environment or a nature lover may help or need help.

3 WHAT BLOCKS YOU

Abundance, or a lack of it, blocks progress. Too much and you cannot identify with the less fortunate. Too little and you resent those with more. Treat health as you would wealth. Your independence or lack of it must be addressed. Your environment or a nature lover may be the problem.

YOUR FOUNDATION

Crucial to your situation is your ability to be self-reliant, independent and free. Learn about Mother Nature's gift of abundance to you. Treat health as you would wealth. Dealing with your environment or the concerns of a nature lover is vital.

WHAT IS BEHIND YOU

In the past, you saw the benefits of being self-reliant and healthy. If you did not apply what you learned, time was wasted. Your independence rests on what you learned. Ecological concerns or those of a nature lover may be waning.

WHAT CROWNS YOU

It would be good to be independent. Visualize yourself in the arms of Mother Nature. See Her give you your share of health and wealth. Know you deserve all She gives you. Vow to regain your connection with Her.

WHAT IS BEFORE YOU

You will soon be able to be independent, self-reliant and free. You will come to know real abundance in a very natural way. Your wealth, health and perhaps your waistline may increase. A nature lover may be involved.

YOUR PERSONA

Present yourself as an independent, self-reliant and natural person. Show you are an abundant source of ideas, inspiration and the valuable wisdom that nature teaches us. Demonstrate the connection between nature and healing.

HOW OTHERS SEE YOU

Others see you as an independent self-reliant and natural person. You seem to be an abundant source of ideas, inspiration and the valuable wisdom that nature teaches us.

YOUR HOPES AND FEARS

You hope you will know abundant health, wealth and the wisdom that nature teaches us, but fear you may not. Your having does not mean there will be less for others. You may fear, or fear for, your independence. Or, you may fear, or fear for, your environment or a nature lover.

THE OUTCOME

You will be able to be independent, self-reliant and free. You will come to know real abundance in a very natural way. Your wealth, health and maybe your waistline may increase. A nature lover may be involved.

Ten of Pentacles

Protection

♦★ Ten of Pentacles:

Protection

1

YOU

You need to make your base secure. Draw support and protection from your past ties and rich family traditions. If you invest conservatively and do not gamble, your success is assured. You may found your own dynasty.

2

WHAT SURROUNDS YOU

You are surrounded by strong support, a rich heritage and protection. You can build on the foundation laid by others. The chance of obtaining much more than you want is real. A protective person or a relative may help or need help.

3

WHAT BLOCKS YOU

Protection, or a lack of it, blocks your progress. Too much? You are kept from important life lessons. Too little? You are wounded and must heal. A well-known name or reputation can be a curse. An over-protective person or relative may be the problem.

Your Foundation

Crucial to your situation is making your base secure. Build on the work and values of those who came before. Then, you may manifest your desires and even more. Protecting and dealing with the protectiveness of others is vital.

What is Behind You

In the past, you saw the benefits of building upon the work and values of others. If you took shortcuts or gambled, time was wasted. Your heritage can help you do well now. The influence of a relative or a protective person may be waning.

What Crowns You

It would be good to be part of a rich tradition. Visualize yourself as one of the first settlers of this land. Feel yourself accepting responsibility for its stewardship. See you are descended from two, from many and from One.

What is Before You

You will soon feel supported and protected by established rules and structures and may use this security to increase your wealth, status and influence. Great wealth can be yours. A relative or a protective person may be involved.

Your Persona

Present yourself as successful, respectful of rich traditions and able to build on what has come before. Show you have been taught by experts and can invest your resources wisely. Be protective of what you hold dear.

HOW OTHERS SEE YOU

Others see you as protective, very successful and respectful of rich traditions. You may remind them of one of their relatives. They think you have been taught by experts, can invest resources wisely and build on what has come before.

YOUR HOPES AND FEARS

You hope that you are going to reach a level of financial security that will endure forever, but fear you may not. You may want wealth and social position, but fear the burdens they require. You may fear, or fear for, a relative or a protective person.

THE OUTCOME

You will feel supported and protected by established rules and structures and may use this security to increase your wealth, status and influence. Great wealth can be yours. A relative or a protective person may be involved. You may found a dynasty of some kind.

Practicality

Princess of Pentacles

 Princess of Pentacles: *Practicality*

1 YOU

You need to concentrate on the communication of practical matters, useful information and values. Trust your natural instincts. A new business idea is near. Take notes and make lists. Keep records and receipts safe and secure.

2 WHAT SURROUNDS YOU

You are surrounded by the need to communicate useful information and practical values. A new business idea is near. Surround yourself with beautiful things. A practical or earthy person may help or need help.

3 WHAT BLOCKS YOU

Being too practical or being impractical blocks your progress. Ignoring emotion, intuition, and imagination is very impractical. Being frivolous gains you nothing. A new business idea or an overly-practical person may be the problem.

YOUR FOUNDATION

Crucial to your situation is appreciating and communicating useful information. A new business idea can become real if a plan is made and followed. Dealing with the practicality and earthiness of a young person is vital.

WHAT IS BEHIND YOU

In the past, the communication of values, useful information, or a new business idea were major issues. Unless targets were set and met, time was wasted. The influence of a practical or earthy young person may be waning.

WHAT CROWNS YOU

It would be good to communicate practical information and useful techniques. Visualize yourself planting the seeds of your ideas in those you care about. See them grow and flower. A new business idea may come to you.

WHAT IS BEFORE YOU

You may soon encounter or have to act as someone who is involved in the communication of practical information and useful techniques. A new business idea may come to you. You may make a proposal for one. An earthy person may become important.

YOUR PERSONA

Present yourself as concerned with the communication of practical information and useful techniques. Do not be afraid to get dirty. Show you are focused on gain, not glamour, and like to do honest work.

How Others See You

Others see you as concerned with the communication of practical information and useful techniques. You seem to enjoy getting your hands dirty and the sweat of honest labor. Some may think you move too slowly.

Your Hopes and Fears

You hope you can learn or teach practical information and useful techniques, but fear you may not. You may fear hard work, getting dirty or ordinariness. You may fear, or fear for, a new business idea or an earthy person.

The Outcome

You may encounter or have to act as someone who is involved in the communication of practical information and useful techniques. A new business idea may come to you. You may make a proposal for one. An earthy person may become important.

Prince of Pentacles

Reliability

◆ Prince of Pentacles:

Reliability

1

YOU

You need to be a part of the implementation of a new business idea. Be trustworthy, reliable and a good provider. Speak seriously and only if you have something to say. Beware of being preoccupied with gain and possession.

2

WHAT SURROUNDS YOU

You are surrounded by the need to conduct business in a serious, reliable and trustworthy manner. There may be a fixation on wealth. A new business may be starting up. A reliable person may help or need help.

3

WHAT BLOCKS YOU

Reliability, or a lack of it, blocks progress. Blind obedience stifles creativity. Unreliability makes it impossible to trust, plan or feel secure. The implementation of a new business plan or an earthy person may be the problem.

YOUR FOUNDATION

Crucial to your situation is your ability to implement a new business plan correctly. Be reliable and consistent. Stick to your position. Focus on the practical aspects of the situation. Dealing with the reliability of a young person is vital.

WHAT IS BEHIND YOU

In the past, you saw the result of implementing a new business idea. If you did not conduct yourself in a serious and reliable manner, do so now. Excitement about a new business or the influence of a reliable person may be waning.

WHAT CROWNS YOU

It would be good to conduct yourself in a businesslike and reliable manner. Visualize the needs of your situation as if you were your own manager, ready to take care of them all in the most practical manner possible.

WHAT IS BEFORE YOU

You will soon encounter or have to act as a reliable, dependable provider. A new business may start up. You may have to say and do whatever it takes to get the job done. A reliable young person may be involved.

YOUR PERSONA

Present yourself as a serious, reliable and businesslike person who wants to fit in and do well. Show your love of the physical world's beauty and riches. Speak slowly and carefully. Show you know how to grow a business.

HOW OTHERS SEE YOU

Others see you as serious, reliable and businesslike. You seem to love the rewards of the physical world. Most see you know how to grow a business. Some see you as too stubborn or addicted to possessions and wealth.

YOUR HOPES AND FEARS

You hope to be reliable, but fear you may not fulfill your commitments in the long run. You may fear you are bad at business, unimaginative, too stubborn or boring. You may fear, or fear for, a reliable young person.

THE OUTCOME

You will encounter or have to act as a reliable, dependable provider. A new business may start up. You may have to say and do whatever it takes to get the job done. A reliable young person may be involved.

Good Fortune

★ Queen of Pentacles

♦ Queen of Pentacles:

Good Fortune

1 YOU

You need to protect your good fortune and that of those you care about. Parties that provide you with social connections can greatly benefit you. Patronize the arts and enjoy your riches as best you can. It will pay off.

2 WHAT SURROUNDS YOU

You are surrounded by the ability to protect your good fortune and that of those you care about. Social connections can greatly benefit you. Patronize the arts and enjoy your riches. A wealthy person may help or need help.

3 WHAT BLOCKS YOU

Good fortune, or a lack of it, blocks progress. See how the unfortunate live or risk forfeiting your humanity. Lack of good fortune sows doubt and weakens resolve. A wealthy person or a pretender to wealth may be the problem.

Your Foundation

Crucial to your situation is protection of your good fortune and that of those you care about. Social connections can greatly benefit you. Patronize the arts and enjoy your riches. Dealing with the ways of a wealthy person is important.

What is Behind You

In the past, you learned the costs and benefits of protecting your good fortune and that of those you care about. Apply what you learned then to the present situation. A wealthy person's influence may be waning.

What Crowns You

It would be good to protect your good fortune and that of those you care about. Visualize yourself as the ruler of your kingdom, able to use your power and influence to easily do so. See your associates wanting to help.

What is Before You

You will soon encounter or have to act as someone who knows how to protect your good fortune and that of those you care about. Patronizing the arts or attending parties may provide you with social connections. A wealthy person will be important.

Your Persona

Present yourself as protective of your good fortune and that of those you care about. Show you have power and influential connections. Be a patron of the arts. Do not be afraid to enjoy your wealth. You have earned it.

How Others See You

Others see you as protective of your good fortune and that of those you care about. They see your power and influential connections. You seem to have earned your wealth. A few petty people think you are snobbish and vain.

Your Hopes and Fears

You hope to be able to protect your good fortune and that of those you care about, but fear you may not be able to. You may fear becoming like someone you used to dislike. You may fear, or fear for, a wealthy person.

The Outcome

You will encounter or have to act as someone who knows how to protect your good fortune and that of those you care about. Patronizing the arts or attending parties may provide you with social connections. A wealthy person will be important.

Pragmatism

◆★ King of Pentacles

★ King of Pentacles:

Pragmatism

1 YOU

You need to be pragmatic and play the political game well. Interact comfortably with everyone, no matter what their status. Get down to basics. Learn to be natural by watching the ways of animals. Working with your hands benefits you.

2 WHAT SURROUNDS YOU

You are surrounded by pragmatism and politics. There is the need to get down to basics. Though there may be a lack of sophistication, the chance for financial gain is very real. A pragmatic person may help or need help.

3 WHAT BLOCKS YOU

Pragmatism, or a lack of it, blocks progress. Lack of political skill or sophistication limits you. Ignoring hard facts because they are inelegant is folly. An overly pragmatic or stubborn person may be the problem.

Your Foundation

4

Crucial to your situation is your ability to be pragmatic and play politics. Interact well with all you meet, no matter what their status. Get down to basics. Be kind to animals. Learn business math. Dealing with the skills of a successfully pragmatic person is vital.

What is Behind You

5

In the past, the ability to be pragmatic and play politics was tested. It was necessary to interact well with everyone. The results of that test must be applied now. The influence of a pragmatic person may be waning.

What Crowns You

6

It would be good to be pragmatic and deal well with the political realities you face. Visualize yourself interacting well with all you meet, learning from them and gaining their support. Realize that this is a spiritual way to live.

What is Before You

7

You will soon encounter or have to act like a person who knows how to be pragmatic and play politics. Go by your basic instincts. You may be helped by an earthy, wealthy deal-maker, and learn how to become one yourself.

Your Persona

8

Present yourself as a pragmatic, expert politician. Act as if you have it all together. Pay attention to budgets and numbers. Show you love good food, nature, sports and animals. Interact well with all you meet, no matter who.

How Others See You

Others see you as a pragmatic, expert politician. You seem to have it all together. You interact well with all you meet. You may be too earthy for some, but all know you are a valuable friend and a fierce enemy.

Your Hopes and Fears

You hope that the persona of a rich and powerful, pragmatic, expert politician will help you attain your goals, but fear it may not. You may fear being liked for what you possess. You may fear, or fear for, a pragmatic person.

The Outcome

You will encounter or have to act like a person who knows how to be pragmatic and play politics. Go by your basic instincts. You may be helped by an earthy, wealthy deal-maker, and learn how to become one yourself.

How does the Tarot "work" when it seems to answer questions so directly?

The nearest thing to an explanation of why the tarot works is an ancient theory held by many peoples throughout the world and rediscovered in the twentieth century by the legendary psychologist, Dr. Carl Jung. His theory of synchronicity (from the Greek *syn* meaning "together" and *chronos* meaning "time") proposed that events happening at the same moment had a relationship of significance.

In other words, when you ask your question with sincerity and you intend to get an answer, you will get an answer, possibly in many ways. It depends on how good you are at deciphering the events around you at the moment you ask the question. A flock of birds, cloud formations, or the pattern the wind makes in the trees could hold an answer.

The tarot is a sort of sacred machine devised to respond to your question and freeze your answer as a picture of it in time so that you may decipher it.

The trick is to know how to derive meaning from your deck of tarot cards and that is what Amy and I have done for you in *The Instant Tarot Reader*.

What if I do not like the answer I receive?

When this happens, it is important to look inside yourself and see why you are troubled by the answer you have received. Do you think you would not be able to cope if things turned out the way the tarot cards are suggesting? Do you have the confidence in yourself to believe that you can cope with a wide range of experiences? If not, why not?

Using the tarot to get in touch with your feelings is one of its most important uses.

The wonderful thing about the tarot is that if you get an unfavorable answer, you can ask the tarot for guidance about how to change things for the better. To do so, you can refer to the *one card, three card* or *Celtic Cross* sample questions on pages 14–21 to help you phrase your question so that you are asking how to change things so that they may work out more to your liking.

What if I am not sure what my answer means?

The large majority of the answers you get using *The Instant Tarot Reader* will make it seem as though the cards picked from your Zerner/Farber deck are speaking directly to your question. However, there may be times when the answer you receive does not appear to be specifically answering your question. These are the best times for developing your intuition and your ability to make decisions.

Let your mind "free associate." This term describes the powerful way your conscious mind communicates with your Higher Self, the source of your inner voice. It does so using sym-

You may experience a flash of intuition that can reveal the meaning that was hidden from you only a moment ago.

bols, the language of your subconscious mind and your dreams. Your first impression upon seeing the image(s) of the card(s) you have picked can inspire in your imagination a further series of images connected to and directed by your Higher Self. In the tarot, The High Priestess is the card symbolizing this process.

If you still do not understand, pick The High Priestess card out of the deck and look at it for a moment. Know that she is going to guide you as you place her back in the deck and shuffle it while asking for a clarification of the meaning of your previous reading. Pick one card and then turn to the page listing its meanings. Read [1] **You**, and find out what you need to know.

What is the origin of the tarot?

There is an old joke told about every kind of scholar: put two of them in a room and you will get three opinions. Some say the

The origin of the tarot and even its original purpose is a subject upon which even the most learned scholars cannot seem to agree.

tarot started out as pasteboard pictures of various gods and goddesses used to teach their divine properties to the illiterate and brought to Europe by travelers from India. These travelers arrived when Egypt was all the rage and found it advantageous to be known as "Gyptees." Their descendents are now known as Gypsies.

That theory might account for many people believing the tarot originated in Egypt. However, there are those that claim tarot came from tenth century China, and there are advocates for Hebraic, Islamic, or Indian origins as well. One thing seems certain: the earliest and most complete deck of tarot cards dates from the early fifteenth century, and is said to have been made for the Duke of Milan.

Egypt advocates say it derives from the words *tar* and *ro*, meaning the "Royal Road." Indian advocates like to remind everyone else that the word *taru* means "cards" in Hindu and that *Tara* is the Aryan name for the Great Mother Goddess. Those voting for tarot being a product of the Hebrew culture point to the word *Torah*, their name for the first five books of the Bible. However, remember that one of the areas where the cards first appeared was Milan, in Northern Italy, where there is a river called the *Taro*. Hmm…

Even the origin of the word "tarot" provokes argument.

There are many who believe the first decks were as likely to have been used as a card game as they were for divinatory guidance. There is probably more than a little truth in that. There is a French word, *tares*, that is used to describe the small dot border on playing cards.

The tarot came a long way in the twentieth century. The wisdom of the cards was an irresistible target for great artists, once they no longer were afraid of persecution and ridicule. The tarot attracted both famous artists, like surrealist Salvador Dali, and those undeservedly not so well known, like Pamela Colman Smith, who under the watchful eye of Arthur Edward Waite, created what we now know as the Rider-Waite deck, the most famous tarot deck of the twentieth Century.

Amy Zerner's fabric collage tapestries have been uniquely successful in blending the essence of the fantasy, fine art, and spiritual wisdom of all the nations thought to have originated the tarot.

What is the difference between the Major Arcana and the Minor Arcana?

The tarot may very well have started out as two separate decks: a spiritually-oriented deck whose purpose was religious instruction and divination, and the deck used for gaming and gambling.

The Major Arcana are the first twenty-two cards of the tarot, starting with number 0, The Fool, and going up to number 21, The World. These cards represent the "arcane" or secret spiritual principles of life. We all make the journey from being The Fool, innocent and poised on the threshold of a great cycle of growth and experience, and eventually arrive at The World, our graduation and the culmination of a major period of our life. Between these two cards are the twenty other major stages of growth and learning. Once we have gone through them all, we are ready to start again on our soul's quest for experience and self-knowledge.

The Minor Arcana help us to bring the spiritual wisdom of the Major Arcana down to earth so that we can use it for our benefit on all levels.

The Minor Arcana are the origin of the modern playing card deck. This deck's four suits—Clubs, Spades, Hearts, and Diamonds—are the descendents of the tarot's traditional four suits—Wands, Swords, Cups, and Pentacles. The Joker in a modern playing card deck is a descendent of The Fool.

The cards of the Minor Arcana are not as concerned with spiritual realities as they are with our everyday, earthly reality as human beings.

Can I do a Tarot reading for another person?

Doing tarot readings for your friends is very enjoyable. However, it is usually best to do your readings by yourself when you are first learning. *The Instant Tarot Reader* is designed so that you will learn quickly. Once you do, it is best to start with a trusted friend, preferably one with an open mind. Eventually, you may feel confident enough to read for anyone, anywhere, anytime. Until then, read and remember the answer to the next Frequently Asked Question.

You will soon feel confident enough to try reading for another person.

Can I do a Tarot reading for someone who is not present?

Wait until you are comfortable with *The Instant Tarot Reader* procedure before trying to ask a question for someone who is not with you at the time you are doing the reading. Remember that most people do not understand what the tarot really is—a decision-making tool—and do not have the rest of the information about becoming an instant tarot reader contained in this book. Make sure the person understands what the tarot really is before attempting a reading for someone else. It is too easy to mislead or frighten the uninitiated if this advice is ignored.

The person must be told that the answers they receive are only indications of the way things might be. They must understand that their free will is more powerful than any tarot reading. There is no reading so good that it cannot be invalidated if someone fails to do what is right. Conversely, there is no tarot reading that is so bad that it, too, cannot be invalidated by changing course and doing what is right. The tarot is a very powerful tool, but it is not more powerful than the people asking the questions. We, alone, are responsible for our actions.

Tarot readings are powerful and must be done the way we have indicated in this book.

If you remember and can convey this to those you want to do a reading for, then you can rest assured that the readings you do will help to guide others. You will then be able to have a lot of fun learning about your life and life in general.

It is a tremendous responsibility to do readings for other people but it is one that Amy and I enjoy even more than reading for ourselves, which we do every day.

We would like to thank you for giving us the chance to share the precious gift of the tarot with you, a gift that has enabled us to make our life a work of art and our art a work of life.

ABOUT THE AUTHORS

When artist Amy Zerner met writer Monte Farber in 1974, an enchanted relationship was formed. Since that time the two have married and become the world's foremost designers of interactive divination systems. Since 1988, Amy and Monte have created seven divination systems or self-transformation tools, three children's books, a coffee-table art book, an album of music, and a CD-ROM series, which they refer to collectively as "spiritual power tools." There are over one million copies of their books in print in nine languages.

Amy Zerner is the first and only artist working primarily in fabric to win a major National Endowment for the Arts fellowship grant in the category of painting. Amy's unique talent as an imagemaker results in art that is based on inner visions, dreams, myths, and fairy tales. Her work combines textiles, embroideries, papers, and assorted found objects to create visionary images intended to act as signposts to spiritual growth and healing.

Monte Farber distills the results of years of studying the tarot, mythology, philosophy, astrology and other ancient wisdom into a form easily understood by today's audience. In addition to being a writer, Monte is an inventor, musician, agent, seminar leader, and, of course, interpreter of Amy's images. In his latest endeavor as host of the radio show, "Metaphysically Speaking," Monte shares his experiences and interviews the brightest stars in the New Age.

Through their work together, Amy and Monte have helped people around the globe to make their inner world a more beautiful and empowering place, so that they are better equipped to deal with the frenzied pace of modern life.